Ens, entity, being, exist^ce   Nonentity, nullity, nihility
Essence, quintess^ce quiddity   nonexist^ce noth^g nought
Nature thing substance   void, zero, cypher blank
  course World. frame   empty
  position constitution
Reality, (v. truth) actual   Unreal ideal, imaginary   unsubstantial
  exist^ce — fact.   visionary, fabulous
  course of things, under^y sun   fictitious, supposititious
  extant, present   absent, shadow. dream
                            phantom, phantasm
Positive, affirmative absolute   Negative, virtual, extrinsic
  intrinsic, substantive   potential. adjective
  inherent

To be, exist, obtain, stand
pass, subsist, prevail, lie
— on foot, on y tapis
to constitute, form, compose   to consist of
    scope, habitude, temperament
State, Mode of exist^ce condition, nature, constitut^n habit
Affection, predicament, situat^n posit^n posture place contingency
Circumstance, case, plight, trim, tune, — point, degree
juncture, conjuncture pass, emergency, exigency.

   Mode, manner, style, cast, fashion, form, shape
Strain, way, degree. — tenure, terms, tenor
footing, character, capacity

  Relation, ship affinity, alliance, analogy, filiat^n (v. Connect^n
Reference, about, respect^g regard^g concerning, touching
in point of, as to — pertaining to, belong^g applicable to
relatively, according to

Peter Mark Roget

www.pocketessentials.com

Other Pocket Essentials by the same author:

Freud and Psychoanalysis

Peter Mark Roget

The Man Who Became a Book

NICK RENNISON

POCKET ESSENTIALS

This edition published in 2007 by Pocket Essentials
P.O.Box 394, Harpenden, Herts, AL5 1XJ
www.pocketessentials.com

A CIP catalogue record for this book is available from the British Library.

ISBN 10: 1-904048-64-1
EAN 13: 978-1-904048-64-0

2 4 6 8 10 9 7 5 3 1

Typeset by Avocet Typeset, Chilton, Aylesbury, Bucks
Printed and bound in Spain

PETER MARK ROGET
1779–1869

Contents

Introduction   11

1: Early Years   15

2: Roget Abroad   35

3: From Manchester to Bloomsbury   41

4: Tragedy Strikes   63

5: Epidemics, Phrenology and Physiology   75

6: Roget and the Royal Society   103

7: Roget and his Thesaurus   123

8: Roget's Last Years   139

Further Reading   147

Websites   151

Index   153

Peter Mark Roget

Introduction

Every day thousands of people consult *Roget's Thesaurus*. It has a place on the bookshelves of English speakers around the world. Look in the reference section of any bookshop or the databases of internet booksellers and you will find dozens of current editions of a work that was first published more than a century and a half ago. *International Roget's Thesaurus, Students' Roget's, Roget's 21st Century Thesaurus, Pocket Roget's Thesaurus*. The list goes on and on. The influence of *Roget's Thesaurus* has extended from the work of academic linguists and computer scientists to the dead parrot sketch in *Monty Python's Flying Circus*, in which much of the humour derives from John Cleese running through a list of synonyms for 'dead' that has quite clearly been culled from the famous reference book.

Yet how many of those who consult it stop to consider why that endlessly useful work is called *Roget's Thesaurus*? Of those who know that it owes its name to the man who first devised it, how many know anything more about him? A little investigation shows that Peter Mark Roget was one of the more remarkable men of his day and he achieved much in a long life that stretched from the years when Britain was fighting rebellious colonists in the

American War of Independence to the high Victorian era. He did not even begin seriously to compile the great work of classification which bears his name until he was 70. Before that, the polymathic Roget had already made his own contributions to knowledge in a dozen different fields, from optics and anatomy to mathematics and education. He might well have been surprised if he had been able to discover that his posthumous reputation rests entirely on his thesaurus. No doubt he would have expected that his involvement in medical education would prove to be an equally lasting legacy. Or his books on magnetism, galvanism and physiology. Or his work on visual perception and the scientific paper on persistence of vision, which was to have an impact he could not have suspected on the later development of motion pictures. Or his association with the Royal Society, then as now the country's most prestigious scientific society, of which he was Secretary for more than twenty years. The range of Roget's interests was remarkable and, for the best part of seven decades, he played a leading role in British intellectual and scientific life.

Any list of his friends and acquaintances is like a roll call of the great, the good and the greatly gifted in Britain from the late Georgian period to the high Victorian era. Here is a man who inhaled mind-altering substances with Wordsworth and Coleridge; swapped ideas with James Watt, Jeremy Bentham, Humphry Davy and Michael Faraday; crossed swords with the computer pioneer Charles Babbage and the geologist Charles Lyell. Here is a

man who was often at the cutting edge of nineteenth-
century research into everything from electricity to infectious diseases. Yet today, although his name lives on in the
title of a reference work, the man himself has been largely
forgotten. There has been only one major biography of
him in the last hundred years and that was published in
1970. This book is not an attempt to match the ground-
breaking work of DL Emblen in *Peter Mark Roget: The Man
and the Word*, which remains the definitive life, but it does
try to rescue Roget from the indifference of posterity and
to provide a short survey of his long and richly productive
life.

Early Years

When Peter Mark Roget was born, George III was nineteen years into his sixty-year-long reign. When he died, Queen Victoria was thirty-two years into her even longer period on the throne. During the ninety years he was alive, Britain and the world changed dramatically. At the time he was born, the country was fighting an ultimately unsuccessful war to retain control of its most prized colonies in North America and prophets of doom were proclaiming the end of the nation's greatness. When he died, Britain was the centre of a vast worldwide empire, on the verge of an expansion into Africa that would make it even vaster. In the year of his birth, the first all cast-iron bridge in the world was completed in Shropshire, Captain Cook was killed by natives on a Hawaiian beach and Napoleon's future wife Josephine was married to her first husband, the Vicomte de Beauharnais. In the year of his death, Stanley set off on his journey into Africa in search of Dr Livingstone, the first women's college at Cambridge was founded and the Suez Canal was opened. The railways, unknown until Roget was in his forties, spanned the country, the industrial revolution had forever altered the lives of millions and the population of London, under a million at the time Roget's arrival increased it by one, had swelled to closer to four million. The world of Roget's childhood had largely vanished.

That childhood began in London. Broadwick Street runs through the centre of Soho. It was once known simply as Broad Street (the name changed in 1936) and it was in this largely unremarkable thoroughfare that Peter Mark Roget was born on 18 January 1779. (Broad Street's other major claim to fame is that it was the birthplace of the poet, engraver and visionary William Blake who entered the world in a room in his father's house there in 1758.) His parents, married the previous year, were Jean and Catherine Roget. Jean, born in 1751, came from a family which could trace its residence in Geneva back to the fifteenth century at least and it was in that city that he had made his debut in life. He had moved to London as a young man to act as the pastor of the French Protestant Church in Soho. Catherine was a member of his congregation when they met, the daughter of a Frith Street jeweller named Peter Romilly whose parents had fled from France in the late seventeenth century when Louis XIV's so-called Revocation of the Edict of Nantes had, in effect, made Protestantism illegal in that country. She was also the older sister of Samuel Romilly, a law student at Gray's Inn at the time of his sister's marriage but a man destined to become both an important legal reformer and a major influence on his nephew. [7]

Of his father, Peter Mark Roget was to know little. Only months after the boy's birth, Jean Roget, suffering from tuberculosis, was told by doctors that his life would be severely shortened if he continued to live amidst the smoke and pollution of London. The answer was for the pastor and his wife to leave the city (and indeed England) and to travel to Switzerland, the country in which Jean had been born and in which many of his family still lived. Entrusting the young Peter Mark to the care of his grandfather, the jeweller Peter Romilly, Jean and Catherine Roget journeyed to Geneva and then to Lausanne in the hope that the Swiss air would prove beneficial to the sickly pastor. It soon became clear that Jean was unlikely ever to be well enough to return to England and plans were made to reunite all the family. Just over a year later, the young boy was brought by his uncle, Samuel Romilly, to join his parents in Switzerland. A daughter named Annette was born on 29 April 1783 but Jean Roget's health continued to deteriorate. Exactly a month after his daughter made her debut in the world, he died. Samuel Romilly wrote to his sister to offer the consolations of faith ('He is now assuredly rewarded for his virtues by that God in whom he has always firmly believed') but the truth was that Catherine was faced by difficult circumstances. A young widow left alone with two children, she had been left with little financial support and was far from home. The only solution to her problems was to return to England.

When she first came back to England, together with her four-year-old son and her newly-born baby daughter, Catherine lodged with family but it was not long before what was to be a lifelong characteristic emerged.

Catherine had an inability to settle anywhere permanently. She seemed always to believe that life would be bound to improve for her and her children if she upped sticks and moved on to pastures new. Over the next decade, she and Peter and Annette were living, at different times, in Kensington and Cheltenham, Dover and Rochester and in a number of other small towns scattered around the country from Devon to Derbyshire. In Kensington, for example, the family lodged on and off with the Chauvet family as paying guests for several years and Peter's earliest schooling took place in the academy for young gentlemen established in Kensington Square in 1786 by David Chauvet, another former resident of Geneva.

During the upheaval and turmoil, much of it self-inflicted, that characterised Catherine's life during these years, only one aim remained constant. Peter must receive a sound education. The Huguenot and Protestant community to which she belonged believed profoundly in the benefits of education, both for its own value and as a means to material and social advancement. It was through education that Peter was to succeed in life. Her letters are filled with details of her son's intellectual progress. From the first, it was the sciences rather than the arts that appealed to the young boy. 'Peter ever eager after new studies,' she wrote to her brother when her son was twelve years old, 'has for this while left this world and lived wholly in the Starry regions. He hired Ferguson on Astronomy, and has been copying off tables and making circles ever since. He gave us yesterday a three hours lecture on Astronomy – Nanette and myself (his only auditors) began at last to be quite weary.' It was clear, from an early age, that Peter was destined for some kind of intellectual achievement and was highly unlikely to become a success in any other sphere. 'His mind will, I see, never bend to business except it was nearly connected with books,' his mother acknowledged as her son entered adolescence.

When he was fourteen, the decision was made that Peter should study at Edinburgh University and that he should take medicine as his subject for study. On 4 October 1793, after a leisurely journey northwards which had taken several weeks, mother, daughter and son arrived in the Scottish capital. At the time Edinburgh University was one of the foremost academic institutions in Europe, with a reputation for excellence arguably greater than that of Oxford or of Cambridge. The great age of the Scottish Enlightenment, in which intellectuals from north of the border like David Hume and Adam Smith had gained fame across Europe, was only just over. Yet the renown their presence had brought to Scotland still remained. Edinburgh University had played its own part in the intellectual ferment of the time and the repu- tation of its medical school was particularly strong. Again this was in direct contrast to the English universities, where medical teaching was almost non-existent. At Cambridge, for example, successive holders of the Regius Professor of Physic did not give a single lecture to undergraduates for more than a century.

It was slightly unusual but certainly not unprecedented for someone as young as Roget to enrol as an undergraduate. David Brewster, the scientist and inventor of the kaleidoscope whom Roget came to admire greatly, entered the university in the same year at the even earlier age of twelve. The medical school at the time was filled with the distinguished, the talented and the eccentric. Among the men whose lectures Roget certainly attended was Alexander Monro II. 'I often hear Dr. Monro who reads lectures on Anatomy in the College,' Roget wrote to his uncle Samuel Romilly in December 1793 when he was still a few weeks short of his fifteenth birthday. 'He has a subject at every lecture, which he dissects in the Class: the smell is sometimes offensive, when the dead body has been kept too long, as was the case yesterday.' Monro was a member of a family that treated the university chair in anatomy almost as an hereditary possession. His father had been one of the founders of the medical school in the 1720s and a physician who was renowned throughout Europe. His son, Alexander Monro III, was teaching in the university when Charles Darwin attended lectures there in the 1820s, although Darwin had no time for the third Monro. 'I dislike him & his lectures so much,' he wrote in a letter home, 'that I cannot speak with decency about them. He is so dirty in person & actions.'

James Gregory, the head of the Edinburgh Medical School in the years that Roget was a student, was another professor who had followed his father's footsteps into the university. A combative man, who once attacked a fellow physician with a stick and beat him so badly he was forced to pay a compensatory fine, Gregory was to end his career in disgrace, charged by the Edinburgh College of Physicians with an assortment of misdemeanours and expelled from its ranks. However, in the mid-1790s, when Roget knew him, Gregory was at the height of his powers. Described by a contemporary as 'a curious and excellent man, a great physician, a great Lecturer, a great Latin scholar and a great talker, vigorous and generous, large of stature and with a strikingly powerful countenance', he was a notable figure in Edinburgh life. Men like Monro and Gregory were powerful personalities and they must have made a significant impact on the young and impressionable Roget.

Altogether, Roget, his mother and his sister Annette were to spend five years in Edinburgh. They were not easy times. Catherine was by no means badly off and was receiving regular sums of money from her brother Samuel, whose reputation and prosperity as a lawyer were growing, but she worried constantly about the family's finances. Their social life, as she complained only too regularly, was dull and restricted. (Possibly one reason Catherine received few visitors during one period of several months was that, in all innocence, she had moved into lodgings in a street renowned as a haunt of prostitutes. She was mortified when she realised that many of her neighbours were, as she reported to her brother, 'women of bad character'.) The health of all three of the

Rogets suffered in the cold and damp of Edinburgh but it was Peter, the sun around which the family circled, whose well-being was of prime importance.

In the summer of 1797, he fell seriously ill. 'He lost appetite,' his mother reported, 'grew weaker than ever, coughed a great deal, and began spitting up dreadful matter mixed with blood.' For a woman who had lost her husband to tuberculosis, an illness such as this afflicting her much-loved son must have given her dreadful anxiety. Eventually time and the ministrations of doctors from the university's medical faculty (and possibly Catherine's own faith in a patent medicine known as Godbald's Vegetable Balsam) brought Roget back to health but the danger had been very real.

His illness in the past, Roget was able in the following year to fulfil the examiners' requirements and present the required thesis (his was on the laws of chemical affinity). On 25 June 1798 he was finally awarded his M D degree. He was nineteen years old. At the time of his graduation, few would have considered that he had been a particularly distinguished student but posterity has thought differently. In 2000, as part of the millennium celebrations, Edinburgh University began a scheme to erect plaques on various sites to commemorate some of the outstanding individuals connected with it through the centuries. Roget, together with David Hume, Sir Walter Scott, Sir Arthur Conan Doyle, Thomas Carlyle and others, has been one of those chosen. (Roget's later association with Manchester is also now commemorated by a plaque in

Coupland Street in the city. In London, the city where he was born and where he was to spend most of his working life, there is, sadly, no blue plaque by which Roget can be remembered.) Roget himself was clearly proud to have been a graduate of Edinburgh and continued to have fond memories of his time there. Friends he made at the university, including Lovell Edgeworth, son of a maverick inventor of Irish extraction named Richard Lovell Edgeworth, and Arthur Aikin, later to be a pioneering geologist and mineralogist, continued to be of importance to him in later life. As late as 1864, five years before his death, when he was eighty-five years old, he not only joined a newly founded Edinburgh University Club in London but agreed to serve as one of its vice-presidents.

What was the newly graduated teenage doctor to do? There were plenty of options open to him but, in the event, Roget made the decision to travel down to Bristol and to involve himself with an establishment that might have been thought by some to be on the fringes of respectable medicine. For a man whose future career was to be, in most respects, a monument to faith in establishment values, it was a curious choice of first job. The Pneumatic Institution for Inhalation Gas Therapy had been founded by Thomas Beddoes in Clifton in 1798, largely using money donated by the Wedgwood family. With apparatus for producing and inhaling gases designed by a friend of Beddoes, the famous engineer and pioneer of steam power, James Watt, the Institution was at the cutting edge of late eighteenth-century medical research.

(Its buildings still stand in Dowry Square, Hotwells in Bristol, although they are now private residences.)

Often portrayed as an eccentric figure, both during his lifetime and by posterity, and now best remembered, if at all, as the father of the morbidly romantic poet Thomas Lovell Beddoes, the founder of the Pneumatic Institution deserves better. Unconventional he certainly was but he was also an imaginative and creative thinker. Beddoes was born in Shropshire and educated at Oxford, where he was briefly Reader in Chemistry before his expressed sympathies with the French Revolution caused such trouble with the university authorities that he chose to resign the post. As a young physician out of work he became interested in the possible therapeutic qualities of natural gases first mooted by the famous chemist Joseph Priestley. The Pneumatic Institution was the result of this interest. It opened to offer outpatient treatment, as an advertisement in the Bristol Gazette stated, to 'persons in Consumption, Asthma, Palsy, Dropsy, obstinate Venereal Complaints, Scrofula or King's Evil, and other diseases which ordinary means have failed to remove'.

Clearly, Beddoes believed in the almost universal efficacy of his therapy. His institution was soon attracting the curious attention of many people, both inside and outside the medical profession. The young poets Samuel Taylor Coleridge and William Wordsworth, who were both living in the West Country at the time, were fascinated by the work in Dowry Square and proved ready volunteers for experimentation. So too did another poet, Robert

Southey, who had been born in Bristol. All three were eager to experience the effects of inhaling the gas nitrous oxide on the imagination and the intellect. In all likelihood, Roget would have met them all. Wordsworth and Coleridge, recently launched on their careers by the appearance of their co-authored book *Lyrical Ballads* (first published in Bristol in 1798), were familiar figures in the city's intellectual circles and in Dowry Square. Coleridge and Southey, like Roget, contributed anonymously to a book about the researches there.

The attention the Institution received was not always desirable. Dowry Square was often the scene of activity designed to scandalise the more respectable inhabitants of Clifton. Joseph Cottle, friend and publisher of Wordsworth and Coleridge, described one such occasion. 'Beddoes persuaded a courageous young lady to breathe out of his pretty green bag this delightful nitrous oxide,' Cottle recorded, and, 'after a few inspirations, to the astonishment of everybody, the young lady dashed out of the house, when, racing down the square, she leaped over a great dog in the way, but being hotly pursued by the fleetest of her friends, the fair fugitive, or rather the temporary maniac, was at length overtaken and secured without further damage.'

Yet, amidst such escapades, the work went on. Beddoes was not only talented and imaginative himself. He recognised the same qualities in others and it is entirely to his credit that he employed the young Humphry Davy, destined to be one of the greatest scientists of the nineteenth century. Davy, only a year older than Roget, had been born in Penzance and came to Beddoes' attention when he was serving an apprenticeship to a local apothecary and surgeon. Recommended to Beddoes by Davies Gilbert, later to be President of the Royal Society when Roget was its Secretary, Davy was appointed as an assistant at the Pneumatic Institution while still in his late teens and, by the time Roget was visiting Dowry Square, he had become the main driving force behind its research.

This research involved almost any gas on which the pneumatic experimenters could lay their hands and was often conducted at great personal risk. Davy was a particularly reckless self-doser and some of his experiments had extremely unpleasant effects on his system. (It is almost certain that his youthful drug-taking contributed to his later death at the comparatively early age of fifty.) One inhalation, he later wrote, 'produced a spasm of the epiglottis so painful as to oblige me to desist instantly. When I opened my lips to inspire common air, nitric acid was instantly formed in my mouth, which burnt the tongue and palate, injured the teeth and produced an inflammation of the mucous membrane which lasted some time.' Unsurprisingly, Davy made a note that, 'I never design to repeat so rash an experiment.' The real star gas of all these experiments, however, continued to be the nitrous oxide which had intrigued the poets and caused the young lady to skip uncontrollably through the streets of Clifton.

Although Beddoes was the first to describe in print the

results of inhaling nitrous oxide (in a pamphlet published in 1799), it was Davy who was in the forefront of the experimentation into its physiological properties. It was he who termed it 'laughing gas' because of the euphoric effects that people experienced when they inhaled it. And it was Davy who published a book in 1800, with the resounding title of *Researches, Chemical and Philosophical; Chiefly Concerning Nitrous Oxide, or Dephlogisticated Nitrous Air, and its Respiration*, which brought the subject to a larger audience. Davy's book included reports by many of the individuals who had taken the gas, including Coleridge who described inhaling it as 'the most unmingled pleasure I ever had'. More importantly, Davy recognised that nitrous oxide had the potential to do even greater good than providing a poet with unmingled pleasure. He realised that because the gas 'appears capable of destroying physical pain, it may probably be used with advantage in surgical operation in which no great effusion of blood takes place'. It is one of the tragedies of early nineteenth-century medicine that Davy, a chemist and scientific researcher rather than a physician, did not follow up on this insight and that no doctor in the next forty years did so either. The history of anaesthesia might have been different.

It was through these two remarkable men, Beddoes and Davy, that the twenty-year-old Roget made his first two appearances in print. A four-page report entitled 'Observations on the Non-prevalence of Consumption Among Butchers, Fishermen etc.' was published in

Beddoes' 1799 book *Essay on the Causes of Pulmonary Consumption* and the reports from medical men in Davy's book of the following year included Roget's description of his experiences with nitrous oxide. They were less positive than those of many of the experimenters. Unlike Coleridge, Roget took little pleasure from inhalation. 'I felt myself totally incapable of speaking, and for some time lost all consciousness of where I was, or who was near me. My whole frame felt as if violently agitated,' he wrote. 'I thought I panted violently; my heart seemed to palpitate, and every artery to throb with violence; I felt a singing in my ears; all the vital motions seemed to be irresistibly hurried on, as if their equilibrium had been destroyed, and everything was running headlong into confusion. My ideas succeeded one another with extreme rapidity; thoughts rushed like a torrent through my mind, as if their velocity had been suddenly accelerated by the bursting of a barrier which had before retained them in their natural and equable course.' For romantic poets, this may have been an exhilarating experience. For a man of science who prided himself throughout his life on his rationality, it was profoundly disturbing. Rather priggishly, the young Roget concluded that, 'I cannot remember that I experienced the least pleasure from any of these sensations.'

Bristol and Beddoes were all very well and they had provided Roget with a fascinating and unconventional start to his career but it was London that offered the young physician the greatest opportunities, as those who thought of themselves as his mentors realised. Etienne Dumont was an old friend of Roget's father and had remained a source of great support to his friend's widow during the difficult years when she had toured Britain from Cheltenham to Edinburgh in search of a suitable place to live. Dumont, born like Roget's father in Geneva, was a well-travelled and well-connected intellectual who had spent periods of his life in St. Petersburg, London and Paris. He had been a friend of the French Revolutionary leader Mirabeau, and had written speeches for him, and he had acted as the editor and translator for French editions of the writings of Jeremy Bentham. Dumont was in no doubt where Roget's future should lie. 'Peter must present himself,' he wrote to Catherine in December 1799, 'he must make connections; he must profit from a stay in the Capital where ideas are in circulation far more than in Bristol or in Cheltenham... London – London! That is the great gate of salvation.'

The great gate swung open through the good offices of Dumont and of Roget's equally well-connected uncle, Samuel Romilly. When the young physician finally journeyed to London in the autumn of 1800, he had an invitation to stay with Jeremy Bentham, a close friend of Romilly and the man whose work Dumont had translated into French. Bentham was one of the most celebrated intellectuals of the day. He was born in Spitalfields in 1748 and is best known today as the advocate of the philosophical doctrine known as utilitarianism (the ethical belief that the highest good is whatever brings the greatest happiness to the greatest number of people) and for the fact that his preserved body (what he called his 'auto-icon') is, as he requested in his will, on public display in the main building of University College, London. However, he was a man with a restless and wide-ranging mind who was interested in everything from the design of prisons to animal rights. Throughout his long life, he was also involved in a number of what today we would call 'scientific' investigations and experiments. It was one of these to which Roget was invited to contribute.

Bentham had been toying with the idea of what he called a 'Frigidarium' – 'a sort of ice house, for the purposes of preserving fermentable substances of all sorts, from prejudicial fermentation, by excluding the degree of heat necessary to that process', as he described it in a letter. Bentham intended to have a Frigidarium built in the garden of his house (on a site now occupied by the Home Office in Queen Anne's Gate) and he wanted the young Roget to investigate the practicality of the project and to undertake the detailed calculations that would be needed to make the ice-house work.

The opportunity to work with such a distinguished man must have seemed an exciting one and Bentham was flatteringly eager to involve the young, only recently graduated physician. Inviting Roget for what would become a six-week stay at his home, Bentham wrote how much he felt 'the want of a confidential friend, whose sympathetic zeal might animate my languor'. Yet, despite what the philosopher said, his languor was not to be so easily animated. His commitment to the project was fitful and Roget's disillusionment with Bentham, as a man 'not calculated to finish what he starts out to do', was rapid. The idea of the Frigidarium was a good one and, in a time of war and food shortages, the benefits of a method of storing food for long periods of time were clear. As an economic proposition, if nothing else, freezing food offered great opportunities. Bentham himself noted that 'the same peach or parcel of green peas which at one time may be had for a shilling, shall another time only by being a few months or even weeks earlier, fetch a guinea'. Unfortunately, the philosopher's projects were too many and too various for him to concentrate on just the one. Roget, growing frustrated at the lack of progress on the Frigidarium, soon withdrew from it. It was never properly constructed. Refrigeration had to wait for more than half a century to become a reality.

Roget's experiences in his first months in London were like those of many young men from the provinces arriving in the capital with a desire to establish themselves and to make their names. He lived frugally and moved frequently from lodgings to lodgings. (One set of lodgings proved unsuitable because, as he reported to his mother, the landlady 'gets drunk regularly every evening, and often the mornings too'.) After parting company from Bentham and the Frigidarium, he struggled to find gainful employment and was delighted to earn five guineas by translating a thesis from English into Latin, even though it was written in 'the most barbarous and most unintelligible style I've ever seen'. He indulged in occasional mild dissipations like attending a New Year's Ball, where the dancing went on until the early hours of the morning, and visiting the theatres in Covent Garden and Drury Lane. (He records seeing performances of *The Merchant of Venice*, *King Lear* and *Othello* but gives little indication of what he thought of any of them.)

However, despite these minor pleasures, Roget was not happy in the city. He wrote at least one self-pitying letter to his mother, then living in Sidmouth, in which he acknowledged that, 'I detest London as cordially as you do' and, by June 1801, he had joined her and his sister in the Devon resort. Whether his new surroundings were any more congenial than the capital is doubtful. Only two months before he arrived, his sister Annette had written to inform him that, 'Sidmouth grows every day more stupid, and the few parties here are extremely unpleasant'. So bored had she become by Devonshire life that she had been obliged to take desperate measures and to seek entertainment in reading through *Encyclopaedia Britannica* volume by volume.

It was time once again for Roget's elders to confer about his future. Advice arrived in letters from his uncle who recommended that Roget should smarten his dress ('not for me but for those who think dress more important than I do, which is almost all the world, or at least that part of the world which you will have to do with') and avoid depressive thoughts ('I know that gaiety is not to be put on like one's coat, but I know by experience that melancholy may be very much increased by being indulged'). As his mother, uncle and friends like Etienne Dumont exchanged ideas about what the immediate future should hold for the newly graduated Roget, a consensus emerged. It was decided that he should tour the Continent and, again through Samuel Romilly's wide range of contacts, he was introduced to John Philips, a wealthy millowner in Manchester who had two young sons needing a tutor to accompany them on an educational tour around Europe. Roget agreed to travel northwards to visit his prospective employer, stopping briefly near Birmingham where he renewed his acquaintance with James Watt, first encountered at the Pneumatic Institution.

Manchester in the first years of the nineteenth century was at the beginning of its transformation into one of the powerhouses of the industrial revolution. In the middle of the eighteenth century, it was a small country town with a population of little more than 20,000. Fifty years later many of the mills and textile factories that were to provide its prosperity had been built and its population had topped 100,000. The town's age-old systems of civic government were struggling to cope with such a large influx of people. Public health provision was woefully inadequate, cheap and jerrybuilt housing had sprung up for the thousands drawn in to work, in often appalling conditions, in the new mills. Manchester was both seething with vitality and scarred by the most wretched poverty. Roget was not impressed by the place when he first saw it. 'The town itself is horrible,' he wrote, 'dirty and black, paved only with small stones, the air always heavy by the smoke of the factories.' However, he did approve of John Philips, one of the more humane and philanthropic employers in the area, and the millowner was clearly impressed by the young physician. He was not only willing to entrust his two sons, Burton and Nathanael, to Roget's care, he was prepared to pay the young man £400 a year to look after them. The great adventure of Roget's life was about to begin.

Roget Abroad

Roget and his two charges set sail from Dover in February 1802. After a terrible crossing to Calais, which took fifteen hours as opposed to the usual four, the three of them set off for Paris. There was peace between France and England for the first time in nearly a decade (the Treaty of Amiens was finally signed in the month after their departure from Dover) and Roget and the two Philips boys were among thousands of English travellers who had taken the opportunity to visit France which had been denied them for so long.

Despite his own Continental ancestry and the fact that he was bilingual in French and English, Roget was, like so many Englishmen, distressed by his first encounters with foreignness. 'The French are very awkward in all their contrivances,' he noted with priggish disdain. He found much to dislike, from the shortage of goods in the shops and the lack of foot pavements in the Parisian streets to the fact that so many of the men he saw on those streets didn't shave often enough to meet with his approval, and three months in the French capital did little to improve his opinion of the city. He was prepared to admit that 'nothing can exceed the magnificence of the Tuileries and the Louvre' and, standing amidst the crowds that lined the streets, he had the opportunity of seeing Napoleon, the man who had upset the balance of power in Europe, as he took part in a state procession to Notre Dame. Otherwise his letters home suggest that it was with something of a sigh of relief that he and the two Philips boys left Paris in May 1802 to travel south towards Geneva, the city in which his father had been born. Accompanying them was Lovell Edgeworth, brother of the novelist Maria Edgeworth, brother-in-law of Thomas Beddoes and an old friend of Roget from his days in Edinburgh.

As they journeyed southwards, they passed through Lyon, a city which had been devastated by the events of the past few years and which had been the scene of a revolutionary reign of terror only marginally less bloody than the one in Paris. Roget was profoundly shocked by what he saw in Lyon where the consequences of the Revolution were more immediately obvious than they had been in the French capital. 'The town itself must have been very fine before the Revolution,' he wrote, 'but all its days of prosperity are now past. No part of France has suffered more from the turbulence and barbarity of the times; the direful effects of the Revolution are everywhere visible. Many of the finest parts of the town lie heaps of ruins.' Roget's own rational, optimistic, Enlightenment view of the world and his belief in the onward march of human progress were shaken, if not entirely undermined, by the evidence of irrationality and destruction before him. 'Events like this are enough to shake to its foundation our confidence in the course of things, and by making us distrust all views into futurity, teach us to confine them to present and more immediate concerns,' he confessed. His confidence in the course of things was due to take some further blows before he was safely back in England.

In the first week of June 1802, the party arrived in Geneva and took lodgings with David Chauvet, an old friend of the Roget family and the man who had once run the school in London's Kensington Square which Roget had attended as a child. They settled down to an agreeable life of study, socialising and sightseeing which was to last for more than six months. Accompanied by a famous guide named Jacques Balmat, reputedly the first man to climb Mont Blanc, they made excursions into the surrounding mountains. However, in February 1803, this idyll was interrupted by the illness and sudden death of Chauvet. The death of their host, with the sorrow and upheaval it brought, was but the first of a series of increasingly difficult problems to face the English visitors in the early months of the year.

Despite the signing of the peace treaty at Amiens, war was once again on the horizon. The prospect of the renewal of hostilities between England and France threatened to strand Roget and his two young charges in what would be enemy territory. Geneva was not then part of Switzerland but an independent city-state that had been effectively annexed by Napoleonic France. As the international situation grew graver, so did the dangers for English citizens staying in Geneva. Plans of escape from the city were concocted by Roget and his friends, some more likely to succeed than others. Roget himself described one of the more cloak-and-dagger attempts to exit Geneva in disguise. 'I was to walk out of the town,' he wrote, 'shabbily dressed in my greatcoat, old hat, crab stick, dark pantaloons, and red handkerchief around my neck, wearing my night shirt without a frill and a dirty waistcoat.' Probably luckily, this subterfuge was abandoned, as were several other plans, and Roget, Burton and Nathanael stayed put for the time being. However, events were beginning to overtake them. At a party, the famous author and arbiter of literary taste Madame de Staël, then resident in the town, warned the young man that there were definite plans afoot to arrest the English in Geneva. At this point, Roget began to reflect on his own family background. Had not his father, who had died when his son was only four years old, nonetheless been born in Geneva? A scheme was developed for Roget to claim Genevan and thus French citizenship and frantic attempts began to get the right documentation to prove that his father had indeed been born in the town.

Burton and Nathanael Philips, under age and thus not threatened by the same restrictions as other English citizens, were sent to Neuchâtel in neutral Switzerland. The search for proper documentation for Roget had been successful and, newly established as a French citizen, he escaped the fate of other Englishmen in Geneva who were arrested and despatched to Verdun. His friend Lovell

Edgeworth was not so lucky. He and his manservant were to remain interned in France for the next eleven years until the collapse of Napoleon's regime finally brought them their release.

Eventually Roget obtained a passport which enabled him to leave Geneva and join the Philips boys in Neuchâtel. In the comparative safety of the Swiss town, he could release his feelings about his treatment. Roget had been given a bad fright as an over-the-top entry in his diary reveals. 'Thank God I have at length escaped from their clutches! The Tygers of Africa are less to be dreaded, are less ferocious than these. Monsters vomited up from the deep are less terrible. Demons commissioned from Hell to execute some infernal purpose... are milder and more to be trusted than they. The land is blasted which they tread upon. The air which blows from their accursed country is loaded with infection. All is blighted and corrupted by their envenomed touch.'

In truth, he had escaped, as he later discovered, a future that might have been even grimmer than that of Edgeworth. The Commandant in Geneva, General Dupuch, had decided that, if Roget was now French, he was liable to conscription into the French army. Had he not travelled to Neuchâtel, he might have found himself unwilling cannon fodder serving Napoleon's grand ambitions. Even in Neuchâtel, Roget and the two adolescents were not yet entirely safe and it was only after a hazardous journey through the Swiss countryside, disguised as peasants, that the three of them crossed the Rhine into

German territory. 'It is impossible to describe the rapture we felt in treading on friendly ground,' Roget wrote. 'It was like awaking from a horrid nightmare.'

Supported by funds arranged by Philips Sr, the three travelled via a roundabout route through assorted German principalities. In Frankfurt, Burton Philips fell ill with 'brain fever' and became, as Roget reported to his uncle, 'completely deranged in his mind'. It was only after treatment by Roget and Dr Samuel Thomas von Soemmerring, a well-known physician and friend of Goethe, that Burton recovered and the three were able to resume their journey. At the end of October they reached the port of Husum in Schleswig Holstein where, after a final, nerve-wracking delay of three weeks, they boarded a ship for England. On 22 November 1803, they arrived in Harwich and, as Roget himself recorded, 'lodged at an inn whose landlord bore the singularly appropriate name of Mr John Bull'.

From Manchester to Bloomsbury

Safely home in England, with the English Channel between him and any plans to conscript him into the French army, Roget now had time to consider again what his future might be. After a short visit to his uncle in London, Roget journeyed to Manchester and the Philips' home, arriving there on 10 December 1803. Once the two Philips brothers were safely returned to the care of their parents, Roget was a free man and he spent the winter in what he called the 'tranquil and sequestered vales of Devonshire', staying with his mother and sister in Ilfracombe.

For much of the following year, Roget was a peripatetic figure, travelling around the country with, it seems, no fixed plan of what to do next. From Ilfracombe, he returned to Manchester for a short stay in April 1804. After a brief sojourn in Edinburgh, where he was initially planning further study at the university, Roget then hurried south to Bath to take up a position as private physician to Lord Lansdowne, a former Prime Minister. Arranged by Etienne Dumont, who had known Lansdowne for twenty years, this was also to prove a temporary solution to Roget's employment problems. By the autumn of 1804, he had once again returned to Manchester and had taken up his first major professional position as a physician in the Public Infirmary there.

The city was an obvious place in which to launch his career as a physician. As Roget himself noted, 'The number of physicians at Manchester bears certainly a less proportion to the population than in most other towns. For 100,000 inhabitants, six or seven physicians seems scarcely an adequate number.' The city, with its over-whelming public health problems, needed medical men. Roget also had friends in high places there. John Philips was not only one of the wealthiest and most respected men in the city, he was also Chairman of the Board of Trustees for the local hospital and he had good reason to be grateful to the man who had returned his sons safely home from the dangers of a potential war zone. His patronage and support could be guaranteed to provide the young man with the ideal entrée to Manchester society.

Roget's relatively short residence in Manchester was important to him. Not only did he take his first significant steps in his chosen profession, he also began to give the kind of regular public lectures that he continued to deliver for much of the rest of his life. (A course of lectures he gave to students in 1806 has often been cited as a major contribution to the development of medical education in the city.) And it was in Manchester that he first began to play the kind of roles he was later to take on the larger stage of London. Any idea that the town was an intellectual backwater at the time should be dismissed. It was one of the fastest growing urban areas in Britain and had a rich cultural life in which both arts and sciences flourished. Many of its citizens were men of significant ability and achievement. Thomas Percival, whose death provided Roget with his opening at the Infirmary, had been an author and physician of some note whose correspondents across Britain and Europe had included such major figures as Voltaire and Diderot. John Ferriar, who became Roget's colleague and friend on the staff of the Infirmary, was a doctor of wide learning and reputation whose medical ideas (the concept of isolation wards for infectious diseases, for example) were often ahead of their time. He was a prolific writer whose works ranged from volumes of medical history to an essay on ghostly apparitions (which argued that they were psychological rather than supernatural phenomena) and a satirical poem entitled *Bibliomania*, poking fun at the excesses of wealthy book-collectors.

There was, then, no shortage in Manchester of congenial society and Roget took full advantage of what the city offered. He was involved in the founding in 1806 of the Portico Library, still in existence, a gathering place for the city's intellectuals, and he acted as the library's first Secretary. He also lost no time in joining the Manchester Literary and Philosophical Society, one of the oldest learned societies in Britain, which had been founded in 1781 and which drew its most active membership very largely from the city's physicians and surgeons. Within two years of joining he was acting as the Society's Vice-President. Roget, as his future long involvement with the Royal Society was to prove, was always a willing and tireless administrator, the sort of member societies of all kinds depend upon for their successful survival. During his time in Manchester, Roget must have been a familiar figure in the Society's purpose-built premises in George Street, now at the heart of the city's Chinatown.

His time as Vice-President coincided with one of the most fruitful periods in the history of the Manchester Literary and Philosophical Society and his fellow officers were men of considerable stature and achievement. The President was Thomas Henry, one of the founders of the Society. An apothecary, Henry had made a fortune from the manufacture of an indigestion powder based on magnesium carbonate. Known for the rest of his life as 'Magnesia Henry', he was a man of wide interests who was a friend of the chemist Joseph Priestley and the translator of work by the French savant Antoine Lavoisier. The Secretary was a largely self-taught poly-math who has undoubtedly been the most distinguished of all the Society's members over the two centuries it has existed. John Dalton, sometimes known as 'the father of modern chemistry', belonged to the Society for fifty years. Born near Cockermouth in the Lake District, Dalton moved to Manchester when he was in his twenties to teach mathematics and 'natural philosophy' and remained there for the rest of his life. He joined the

Society soon after he arrived in the city and, only months later, in 1794, he communicated to fellow members the results of his investigations into colour blindness, an affliction from which he suffered himself and which he was the first person to scientifically describe. (For much of the nineteenth century and later, a particular type of colour blindness was usually known as 'Daltonism'.) In 1803, two years before Roget joined the Society, Dalton presented a paper to it in which he described his enquiries into 'the relative weights of the ultimate particles of gaseous and other bodies' – the starting point for research which made Dalton the first great theorist of atomic chemistry. Dalton was a solitary workaholic whose only recreation was said to be a game of bowls every Thursday afternoon at a Manchester pub called the Dog and Partridge but, since they served as officers of the Society at the same time, Roget must have known him as well as almost anybody. The experience of meeting and working with a man of such brilliance can only have been a stimulating one for him.

Despite the young physician's successes in Manchester, his family still worried over his well-being. Although he had suffered no recurrences of the illness that had struck him when he was a student, his state of mind now seems to have been in question. 'Despondency is, I have always thought, the great defect of our family,' Samuel Romilly wrote to his nephew during Roget's time in Manchester, 'and I do not think you are more exempt from it than the rest.' If Roget did suffer from any family predisposition to despondency, then his method of dealing with it, then and later, was to immerse himself in work.

While Roget was in Manchester, his mother and sister continued their peregrinations around the country. From Bangor to Chepstow, from Aberystwyth to Derby, the two travelled from town to town, staying a few weeks or a few months before moving on in search of another place which might suit them better. For much of the time Annette was ill, suffering from an array of physical and psychosomatic complaints. The correspondence his mother sent Roget at this time is filled with a catalogue of the tonics and remedies, from calomel pills and powder of valerian to opium and tincture of castor, with which Catherine was dosing her daughter. Roget replied to his mother's letters, overflowing with the details of largely unsuccessful medical treatments, as best he could but it is hard to avoid the conclusion that the neediness and constant griping of his two nearest relations often exasperated him. It is also difficult to resist the idea that Annette's assorted ailments were more psychological in origin than physical. The most likely explanations for her undoubted suffering during this period is that, sometime during their time in Ilfracombe, Roget's sister had experienced the misery of a failed affair of the heart. In the words of Roget's biographer, DL Emblen, whatever she had undergone, it changed her 'within a few short years from a happy, mischievous young woman into a dour and lonely, often neurotic, spinster'. Emblen goes on to quote lines from a poem Annette wrote in late 1804 which certainly suggest that she had come to have a jaundiced view of courtship and romance as practised at the time:

> I hate your coxcomb beaux who flutter
> And in your ear soft speeches mutter,
> Pretend how much your charms give pain
> And shed false tears like show'rs of rain.
> Oh how I hold such puppies low!
> Their hearts as cold as ice or snow:
> What marry one? Rather than risk it
> I'd live for life on bread and biscuit.

Roget, however close he was to his family, could only spare a little time to address the problems of his mother and his sister. He had his own medical career to consider. Although Manchester was more lively intellectually and scientifically than might at first appear to be the case, London was still the place where a physician like Roget could achieve genuine success. In the late autumn of 1808 he moved to the capital and took up temporary residence in his uncle's house in Russell Square. It was to be a short stay, for the generous Romilly, by now at the peak of his legal career and an important public figure who had served in the short-lived government known as the 'Ministry of All the Talents', had plans for his nephew's future. He purchased a house in Bernard Street, very close to Russell Square, and, at the beginning of 1809, not only was the young physician set up in his first real home but he was also joined there by his mother and sister, who were finally able to end the dreary tours of the small towns and coastal resorts of Britain they had been making for so many years.

In 1809, Bernard Street had just been built on land owned by the nearby Foundling Hospital and it had been named after Sir Thomas Bernard, the Hospital Treasurer from 1795 to 1806. The row of houses which included Roget's new home stood just opposite the entrance to today's Russell Square tube station. It was demolished in the 1960s but very similar buildings, the tall and thin terraces so typical of the area, can still be seen in the streets of Bloomsbury today. It was an ideal place from which to launch a career in medicine and it was to remain Roget's home for forty years.

His first medical jobs in the capital were with the Northern Dispensary and the Great Windmill Street School of Medicine. The Northern Dispensary has been described by one historian as 'the quintessential Victorian expression of medical charity' and Roget was involved in its work from its founding in a street off what is now the Euston Road in June 1810. He gave his services for free in what was then a poor area of the city and continued to do so, even as his own paid practice expanded, for nearly two decades.

The Hunterian School of Medicine, often known from its location as the Great Windmill School of Medicine, had been founded in 1769 by the famous Scottish physi-

cian, obstetrician and anatomist William Hunter. Roget
lectured there on the Theory and Practice of Physic but
the school's primary function was to provide instruction
in anatomy for the capital's trainee doctors and
surgeons. At the time London's hospitals had few facilities for training their own future staff and private
schools like Hunter's filled the gap. It had particularly
close ties with the Middlesex Hospital with which
Hunter himself had been connected. As Etienne Dumont
had once written in a letter to Catherine Roget, 'A
dissection is the most useful book for a doctor', but,
even in a well-established and well-respected institution
like the Hunterian School, bodies were hard to come by.
In theory, the subjects for dissection in the schools were
hanged criminals but demand outran supply and this was
the heyday of the resurrectionists, men who dug up
bodies to sell to the anatomists. In extreme cases, resurrectionists turned to murder. The most infamous
instance of this, still remembered in the nation's folk
memory, was the case of Burke and Hare. They started
their careers as just two of the many seedy individuals
earning a living from the dead, raiding graveyards to get
fresh corpses for hospital dissecting schools, but they
soon decided this was too much like hard work. Why go
to the bother of digging up a corpse when you could just
bump off one of the city's vagrants and miss out on all
the tedious and backbreaking labour of unearthing the
body? They had hurried more than a dozen people
prematurely out of this world and onto the mortuary

slab before they were caught and Burke was executed.

Burke and Hare worked in Edinburgh but London had its own equivalent *cause célèbre* in the 1830s. On 5 November 1831, three of the capital's 'resurrection men' had turned up at King's College in the Strand with the body of a young boy for sale. Richard Partridge, demonstrator of anatomy at the college, was suspicious. The body looked remarkably fresh. Tricking the three men into waiting in the entrance hall of the college, Partridge sent for the police. Under arrest, John Bishop, James May and Thomas Williams insisted that the body of the teenager (later assumed to be an Italian street entertainer called Carlo Ferrari) had been obtained by the usual means. He'd died of natural causes, he'd been buried and they'd come along and disinterred him in order to cart him off for dissection. Nobody believed them and the three men were placed on trial at the Old Bailey for the murder of the Italian boy. All were convicted and, although May was reprieved at the last minute (Bishop confessed after the verdict that May had been ignorant of the murder and had only been helping in the sale of the body), the other two were hanged.

By the time of 'The Italian Boy' murder, the general hospitals had begun to expand their own teaching facilities and the private schools of medicine and anatomy were starting to lose their status and their *raison d'être*. The Hunterian School of Medicine was to survive until 1839. The building has long been demolished and the Lyric Theatre now stands on the site where Roget gave some of his earliest lectures in the capital.

Throughout his life, Roget was a man who relished the company and intellectual stimulation of his peers. He was an inveterate joiner of societies and, from his earliest days in Bernard Street, he was an enthusiastic member of the Medical and Chirurgical Society. Founded in 1805, after a group of largely younger doctors had resigned from the existing Medical Society of London in protest at the autocratic regime of its president, James Sims, the Medical and Chirurgical Society was the distant ancestor of today's Royal Society of Medicine. Roget found congenial company there for many years. He was Secretary of the Society for more than a decade and a regular contributor to its *Transactions*, beginning with a paper entitled 'A Case of Recovery from the Effects of Arsenic, with Remarks on a New Mode of Detecting the Presence of This Metal'. (This was the record of one of Roget's more unusual cases, in which he had been summoned to attend a teenage girl 'of sanguine temperament and delicate constitution' who had 'formed the resolution of putting an end to her existence'. In pursuit of this aim, she had 'purchased 60 grains of white oxyd of arsenic, left her house at 8pm, strewed the powder upon a piece of bread and butter, and eat the whole'.) Roget continued to give his time to the Medical and Chirurgical Society until at least the 1830s, serving several terms as Treasurer, acting as its librarian and classifying its books, arranging the purchase of a house in Lincoln's Inn Fields for its headquarters and, even on one occasion, pursuing a fraudulent employee who had pocketed £335 of the society's funds.

Nearly all the brightest and best of the young medics in London belonged to the Medical and Chirurgical Society and Roget made many friendships there. John Yelloly was five years older than Roget and had been appointed physician at the London Hospital in Whitechapel in 1807. He was one of the founders of the Medical and Chirurgical Society. John Bostock, at the time another up-and-coming physician, was to gain his own peculiar claim to fame in 1819 when, based on his observations of his own health, he became the first person ever to provide a clinical description of hay fever. For much of the nineteenth century, hay fever was often called 'Bostock's catarrh'. Perhaps the most important friendship Roget made, however, was that with Alexander Marcet. Nine years older than Roget, Marcet was, like Yelloly, one of the original members who had seceded from the Medical Society of London in protest at the high-handed authoritarianism of James Sims. He had been born in Geneva and had, like Roget, studied medicine at the University of Edinburgh. The two men certainly knew one another both in Edinburgh and probably earlier, through the Huguenot connection, but it was only now that they became close. Moving to London, Marcet had prospered sufficiently in the city to choose to live there permanently and he had become a naturalised British citizen. He was one of the most diligent members of the Medical and Chirurgical Society and, like Roget, he contributed articles regularly to its *Transactions*.

Probably the most intriguing of these papers, then and now, outlined the bizarre case of an American sailor named John Cummings who had lived for several years after swallowing more than thirty clasp knives and other metallic objects. Cummings had been inspired by witnessing a French circus artist apparently swallowing knives during his act. Later, when drunk, Cummings had boasted to his shipmates that anything a Frenchman could do, an American could do better. When they refused to believe him and had wagered he could not match the feat, he had accepted the challenge and downed four knives. Surviving this one foolhardy experiment, he had proceeded to repeat it some years later, not once but twice. Again drunk on both occasions, he had swallowed a grand total of thirty-four knives. Unsurprisingly, he was soon in hospital suffering from acute abdominal pains and he had eventually died in 1809. Thirteen years later Marcet presented the curious case to his colleagues at the Medical and Chirurgical Society and even had a glass case containing the pieces removed from Cummings' stomach after his death to show them. In all likelihood, Roget was in the audience to hear his friend's account of the medical consequences of the American sailor's rashness.

From the time of their first meeting, Roget found himself drawn into the wider circle of Marcet's family. Jane Marcet, the doctor's wife, was a gifted woman with

a career of her own. Born into another of the wealthy
and intellectually talented families that lived in London
but had their origins in Huguenot France and Protestant
Switzerland, she married her husband in 1799 when she
was thirty. Seven years later she published *Conversations
on Chemistry*, the first of a series of introductory books to
scientific subjects. (Roget was himself to provide Jane
Marcet with help for later books, such as *Conversations on
Natural Philiosophy*, published in 1819, reading her proofs
and making suggestions for improvements to the text.)
Taking the form of a dialogue between a female teacher,
Mrs Bryant, and her two young pupils, Caroline and
Emily, the books proved remarkably successful. Intended
for young people, they proved to have a wider audience.
Through her husband and his wide circle of friends,
including Roget, Jane Marcet was in touch with cutting
edge ideas in the sciences and her books, despite the
simplicity of their format, were up-to-date and, in their
own way, inspiring. One of the greatest of all experimental scientists, Michael Faraday, later claimed that it
was, 'Mrs. Marcet's *Conversations on Chemistry* which gave
me my foundation in that science... I felt that I had got
hold of an anchor in chemical knowledge, and clung fast
to it.'

Other intellectual societies, beyond the Medical and
Chirurgical and outside the confines of Roget's own
particular profession, opened their doors to him. From
March 1812, he was a member of the Royal Institution,
founded in London only a dozen years earlier with the

aim of 'diffusing the knowledge and facilitating the general introduction of useful mechanical inventions and improvements, and for teaching by courses of philosophical lectures and experiments the application of science to the common purposes of life'. Royal patronage from George III was important to the Institution's early success but what really made it into an intellectual powerhouse of the era was the involvement of Humphry Davy, Roget's colleague from Bristol, who was appointed Professor of Chemistry there in 1802, and, later, of Michael Faraday, who began a long association with the Institution the year after Roget joined. Only two months after becoming a member, Roget was invited to deliver a series of lectures at the Institution's lecture theatre in Albermarle Street. Other lecturers in that same year included Davy, Thomas Campbell, a now largely forgotten but then highly esteemed poet, and the botanist and founder of the Linnaean Society, JE Smith. Roget was beginning to move in the upper echelons of British intellectual life and the fact that he was asked to repeat his performances on the lecture stand in subsequent years is an indication of the respect in which he was now held by his peers.

Roget's close ties with the Royal Institution were to continue for many years. In 1834, he was chosen as the first Fullerian Professor of Physiology there. John Fuller (1757–1834) was another of those upper-class eccentrics whose careers enliven the history of England in the late eighteenth and early nineteenth centuries. Known by many as 'Mad Jack' (unsurprisingly, he himself preferred the sobriquet 'Honest John'), Fuller was a wealthy Sussex squire. Entering parliament in 1780, he had a long political career that came to an unfortunate end when he was involved in a drunken altercation with the Speaker and was ignominiously expelled from the House of Commons. At his home in Brightling, Sussex, Fuller enriched the local landscape with a series of architectural follies that still stand today. The Sugar Loaf, a weirdly pointed building that can be seen in a meadow off the road between Battle and Heathfield, was supposedly built in order to win a bet. Fuller had staked money on his ability to see a particular church spire from his house. When he realised that he couldn't, he had the Sugar Loaf built to provide the necessary viewing point. Other constructions which survive to bear witness to Fuller's enthusiasm for offbeat architecture include a sixty-five-foot-high obelisk on the Sussex Downs, a pyramid-shaped mausoleum underneath which he lies buried and a pseudo-Greek temple which stands on a hilltop in what were once his estates.

However, Fuller was much more than just a colourful example of aristocratic oddity. He was a man of genuine culture and achievement, a patron of the painter JMW Turner and a long-time benefactor of the Royal Institution, of which he had been a founder member. Fuller was keen to maintain what he saw as British supremacy in the sciences. 'It never shall be said,' he wrote in an open letter to the Royal Institution, 'that

Britons, who are now at the head of all science, shall at any time shrink beneath the level of the rest of mankind.' He was prepared to put his money where his mouth was. Just before he died, he provided funds for the establishment of two professorships, one in chemistry and one in physiology. The professorship in chemistry was created especially for Michael Faraday whom Fuller much admired and he held it for the rest of his life. The physiology professorship was Roget's for three years. Both posts are still in existence today and, over the years, they have been held by many distinguished scientists. Between 1863 and 1867, for example, Darwin's most effective advocate, the biologist TH Huxley, held the same position that Roget had filled.

It was about the time he started his career as a public lecturer in London, speaking at the Royal Institution and in many other venues, that Roget began to develop an interest in the system of strengthening the memory devised by Gregor von Feinagle, a German monk whose ideas about mnemonics became briefly fashionable at the time. (Von Feinagle was sufficiently well-known to attract the attention of Byron who wrote in his poem *Don Juan* of a character whose memory was so good that, 'for her Feinagle's were an useless art'.) Roget attended lectures von Feinagle gave in London in 1810 and 1811 and bought a book, *The New Art of Memory*, published in 1812, which was based on the monk's ideas. Not only did this demonstrate a practical interest in the subject (who needed a reliable method of training his memory more than a frequent public lecturer?) but it was also an example of Roget's lifelong enthusiasm for schemes of systematising human knowledge. Forty years on, this enthusiasm was to have its longest-lasting embodiment in the Thesaurus.

Feinagle's system echoed ideas about the art of memory which had been current for centuries and advocated the linking in one's mind of particular facts with specific locations. The theory was that, by creating a mental map of rooms or landscapes and filling them with what one wanted to memorise, one would construct unbreakable associations between the visual images and the facts. The anonymous friend who wrote Roget's obituary for the *Proceedings of the Royal Society* bore witness to the fact that he used the method for the rest of his life. 'The houses he lived in, and those of friends he visited, the old rooms of the Royal Society at Somerset House, and of various Institutions which he frequented, were pictured to his mind's eye as peopled with an infinitude of facts, and teeming with varied information. The chronicle of universal history, the measurement of earth and sky, the epochs of his life and those of his contemporaries, the sources of his income, the categories of his Thesaurus, the general arrangement of human knowledge, were all recorded in this manner in the tablets of his memory.'

In 1815 came the culmination of Roget's early immersion in the intellectual life of the capital. He was elected a Fellow of the Royal Society. Founded in the reign of

Charles II, the Royal Society, then as now, was the most prestigious of all scientific societies in the country. With the support of the chemist and physicist William Hyde Wollaston, who held the position of Secretary of the Society that Roget was one day to make his own, the thirty-six-year-old physician was able to show his gifts in another field. Surrounded by evidence of his multifarious talents, it is easy to forget that Roget was also a very good mathematician and it was largely on the strength of a mathematical paper that he was elected to the Society. Entitled 'Description of a New Instrument for Performing Mechanically the Involution and Evolution of Numbers' (involution, in mathematical terms, is raising a number to any power; evolution is extracting any root of a number), Roget's paper showed the means by which a simple slide rule, first invented in the 1620s by William Oughtred, could be modified to allow users to perform calculations involving roots and exponents. A fine example of his mathematical abilities, Roget's modified slide-rule was for a long time regarded as little more than a curiosity but he would live to see its principles re-discovered by a later generation and used by mathematicians and engineers around the world until the progress of electronic computing made it redundant.

The importance of election to the Royal Society was recognised by everyone at the time, not least by Roget himself who, throughout the rest of his life, always carefully placed the three magic initials 'FRS' after his name. He was to stipulate that they should also be placed on his tombstone. They signalled Roget's admission to the inner, governing circle of scientific life, a position he was to maintain and expand over the years to come, but other honours continued to be bestowed on him. In 1816, he was elected a member of the Royal Society of Arts, still flourishing in the impressive building in John Adam Street which Roget would have known. The man who proposed Roget as a member was a younger scientist named John Frederic Daniell, already known as a pioneering meteorologist and later to develop one of the earliest types of battery, the so-called 'Daniell Constant Cell'. Daniell, who may well have met Roget when he attended lectures at the Great Windmill Street School, was to become a long-standing and valued colleague, involved with him in the work of the Society for the Diffusion of Useful Knowledge and Foreign Secretary of the Royal Society between 1839 and 1845. Roget himself much valued his association with the RSA and was to go on to become its Vice-President in 1832 and to hold the post for more than two decades. His career as a physician was also going well. In 1817, he was appointed Consulting Physician to Queen Charlotte's Lying-In Hospital in what is now the Marylebone Road, an institution whose purpose was 'to afford an asylum for indigent females during the awful period of childbirth and also to facilitate the repentance of suffering and contrite sinners'.

In short, as he approached the age of forty, Roget had become a familiar figure in the close-knit intellectual world of medicine and science in London. Both in his professional career as a physician and in his parallel life as a scientist and savant, he had gained recognition from his peers. His own private practice as a doctor had grown to the point where he no longer needed to go in search of patients. They came to him. His financial status and future were secure. However, he was about to face an event that was to prove one of the worst tragedies of his life.

Tragedy Strikes

Sir Samuel Romilly was a major figure in the reform movement of Regency England. Over the years Roget's uncle had become both a highly successful lawyer and a prominent advocate of radical changes in the penal code, arguing that its severity was self-defeating. A system of punishment that involved the death penalty for a vast array of largely petty crimes, he pointed out, was neither just nor workable. In 1806, Romilly was appointed Solicitor-General in the government known as the 'Ministry of all the Talents' and entered parliament. The ministry lasted only a short time in office but Romilly remained an MP for the rest of his life, presenting a series of bills before the House of Commons which aimed to reduce the number of offences for which the death penalty could be invoked. As Romilly himself said in a speech to the Commons, there was 'no country on the face of the earth in which there have been so many different offences according to law to be punished with death as in England'. When death could be the punishment for such diverse activities as begging without a license, blacking one's face at night and cutting down young trees (all of which were, in theory at least, if not in practice, liable to the ultimate penalty) Romilly could see that the law was made a mockery. Only a handful of his bills passed into law but Romilly's eloquence in parliament made him a hero for radical reformers. His importance to Roget, who had lost his father before he had chance to know him and to whom Samuel Romilly had become very much a father-figure, was much more personal. The entire Roget/Romilly family was about to suffer a grievous tragedy. In October 1818 Roget's aunt, Anne Romilly, died after a long illness. A mere four days later, his uncle, distraught at his loss, committed suicide by cutting his throat with a razor. His nephew was present as he died. It is safe to assume that, apart from the death of his wife, it was the most terrible event of Roget's life.

Tragically, the warning signs had been there. Roget's friend Alexander Marcet wrote to him that he had observed Romilly's behaviour during his wife's illness and had been concerned. 'Any symptom of declining firmness of mind,' Marcet remarked, 'is doubly alarming in a man of his stamp.' Romilly himself spoke of his own fears about losing his mind as a result of his anxieties. Throughout the period of his wife's illness, he engaged in frenetic writings and rewritings of the terms of his will. In one codicil, he referred ominously to his worries about his mental well-being. 'I am at the present moment of perfectly sound mind and in the full possession of all my faculties,' he wrote in early October, 'but I am labouring under a most severe affliction and I cannot recollect that insanity is amongst the evils which mortal afflictions sometimes produce without observing to myself that that unhappy lot may possibly be at some time mine.' When Anne Romilly finally died on 29 October 1818, it was Roget who had to face the terrible problem of telling his uncle of her death.

The death had occurred at Cowes, where the couple had been staying with their friend, the architect John Nash, but, immediately after Anne Romilly's death, Roget decided that it would be best for his uncle to travel back to London as soon as possible. Returning the bereaved man to London was not an easy task. During the journey, which took a couple of days, Romilly was obviously deeply distressed and in a pitiable emotional state. Etienne Dumont, his old friend, recorded that, 'He appeared to me to be in the state of a man dying of an internal wound'.

After arrival at Romilly's home in Russell Square, it was agreed that the new widower should not, under any circumstances, be left alone. However, on the afternoon of 2 November, he asked his daughter, who was watching over him in his bedroom, to go downstairs in search of his physician nephew. While she was gone, Romilly got out of his bed, found his razor and slashed his throat. When Roget and a servant burst open the door of the room a few minutes later, he was leaning over the washstand with blood flowing down his chest. He collapsed into Roget's arms and, despite frantic efforts to staunch the wounds, he died shortly afterwards.

Unsurprisingly, Roget was extraordinarily distressed

by his uncle's death. He wrote a short note to Alexander Marcet, admitting that, 'I am almost distracted' and, when an inquest was held, Marcet was obliged to send a statement to the coroner that his friend was in no condition to give evidence. It is surely a measure of the depth of his anguish that, even though Roget must have been one of the most important of witnesses, this was accepted. He was not asked to appear before the coroner. The verdict of the jury at the coroner's court was unequivocal. Despite the fact that this was an age when the supposed stigma of suicide, especially among the 'respectable' classes, was routinely covered up or hidden beneath euphemism, they declared that, 'We are unanimously of opinion that the deceased cut his throat while in a state of mental temporary derangement'.

Roget's agony was made worse by questions and criticism levelled at him over his treatment of his uncle after his wife's death. Was he right to insist that Romilly, clearly in a dreadful state, should travel back to London? Most of all, should Romilly have been left on his own at all, however briefly? Many believed that the nephew had made some severe errors of judgement in the arrangements he had made to look after his uncle. The Whig politician Lord Grey, who had once employed Roget briefly as a private secretary, noted that it 'seems almost incredible' that Romilly 'with such symptoms upon him... should have been suffered to remain one minute alone'. In the end, however, any criticism of Roget among friends and acquaintances was soon enough overwhelmed by sympathy for a man who had lost a much-loved uncle in such tragic circumstances.

Life had, none the less, to go on and Roget was not one to allow personal sorrow to stand in the way of work. His own continued significance in the intellectual life of London over the next few years can be judged by the sheer number of scientific bodies of which he was an active member. He had joined the Geological Society in 1809 and was still a member when he died sixty years later; he was elected a Fellow of the Royal Astronomical Society in 1822; he was a member of the Zoological Society of London from 1827, the year after it was founded and the year before the opening to members of the Zoological Gardens in Regent's Park, until his death; he was a charter member of the Royal Geographical Society, the Royal Entomological Society and the British Association for the Advancement of Science. All the intellectual labour he devoted to societies such as these – all the attendances at meetings, the unpaid secretarial work he undertook for many of them, the papers he wrote and presented at meetings – must have provided a means of forgetting the tragedy that had befallen his family.

Roget also increased his standing in the intellectual world by contributions to the *Supplement to the Fourth, Fifth and Sixth and Sixth Editions* of the *Encyclopaedia Britannica*. Throughout the late 1810s and early 1820s, he had been honing his talents as a writer. He had produced articles for less ambitious reference works than *Britannica*, like *Rees's Cyclopedia*, and, in a magazine with the all-encompassing title of *The Literary Gazette and Journal of Belles Lettres, Arts, Sciences, Etc*, he had published abridged versions of lectures at the Royal Institution on subjects ranging from 'Vision' to 'Molluscs'. By writing for *Britannica*, he had taken a step up the intellectual ladder. Other contributors to the *Supplement* included such prominent names as the economists David Ricardo and Thomas Malthus, the critic and essayist William Hazlitt, and the novelist Sir Walter Scott.

Britannica, first published in three volumes in the years between 1768 and 1771, had gone through several editions in succeeding decades and had already established its reputation as the most comprehensive and reliable reference work in English. The *Supplement* appeared in six volumes between 1816 and 1824 and was designed to fill the gaps in previously published editions. Over the years, Roget wrote hundreds of thousands of words for *Britannica* on subjects that ranged from bee-keeping and phrenology to the teaching of the deaf and dumb and the kaleidoscope. Many of the articles he wrote were still being used in later editions of the encyclopaedia nearly a century after he had written them. Indeed, compressed and edited versions of Roget articles appeared in the *Encyclopaedia Britannica* until very recently. More people will have seen Roget's work in *Britannica* than anywhere else save in the Thesaurus. His most important single work for *Britannica* was the entry he wrote on 'Physiology', a subject on which he was now considered one of the country's leading experts. The seventh edition of Britannica, appearing in successive volumes throughout the 1830s and incorporating much material from the *Supplement*, contained an essay by Roget which ran to more than a hundred and fifty pages and which embodied ideas he had developed over more than twenty years of lecturing and writing on the subject.

At the same time that Roget was devoting so much time to writing for *Britannica*, he also became a founder member of the Society for the Diffusion of Useful Knowledge. The SDUK was in many ways an atypical example of the kind of body to which Roget gave so much of his time. Most of the societies to which he belonged were, in one way or another, professional bodies organised to provide practitioners in the emerging specialist sciences (geology, zoology etc.) with the opportunity to exchange ideas with their peers. The SDUK was different. Its main instigator was Lord Brougham, the Whig politician and lawyer who later became Lord Chancellor. Brougham, who had a long-standing interest in the education of the middle and working classes, saw the society as a means by which knowledge and information could be disseminated to working people. In order to fulfil its announced aim of 'imparting useful information to all classes of the community, particularly to such as are unable to avail themselves of experienced teachers, or may prefer learning by themselves', the SDUK sponsored cheap publications like *The Penny Magazine* and *The Penny Cyclopedia*. Other distinguished men of the time, including Francis Beaufort, the naval officer responsible for the introduction of the Beaufort Scale for measuring wind force, James Mill, philosopher, economist and father of John Stuart Mill and John Cam Hobhouse, MP and friend of Lord Byron, served with Roget on the society's governing committee.

The SDUK did not remain in existence for much more than a couple of decades. Although it sponsored many publications and, at least initially, included so many of the great and the good amongst its subscribers, it did not gain wider and lasting support from those it aimed to educate. By the early 1840s, it was foundering. In 1829, there had been more than five hundred subscribers, wealthy and upper class people prepared to give money for the education of their social inferiors. In 1842, there were less than fifty and the SDUK finally folded six years later. However, during its existence, it had few more diligent supporters than Roget, 'the most eminent of its men of science' as the publisher Charles Knight called him, who wrote tens of thousands of words for its assorted publications.

In his contributions to SDUK publications, even more than in his encyclopaedia entries, Roget became a leading writer of what today we would call 'popular science'. Treatises, published in booklet form, on such subjects as 'Electricity', 'Galvanism' and 'Magnetism', all written by Roget, were the means by which the latest ideas about science were conveyed to a larger audience beyond the small circle of largely London-based scientists and savants. As these titles suggest, Roget was no narrow specialist and he did not confine his work to medicine and mathematics. He was an eager experimenter in electricity and magnetism, subjects which had seized the attention and imagination of many minds in the 1820s and 1830s. Across Europe, researchers were unravelling the mysteries of electrical phenomena. In Denmark, Hans Christian Ørsted had discovered the relationship between electricity and magnetism that we now call electromagnetism. In 1820, the same year that saw Ørsted's most important experiments, the Frenchman André-Marie Ampère developed a mathematical means (Ampère's Law) of decribing the magnetic force between two electric currents. Seven years later, the German scientist Georg Simon Ohm published his own ideas about electrical currents and electrical resistance in a ground-breaking pamphlet. British researchers were not lagging behind their continental counterparts. William Sturgeon, a lecturer in science at the Royal Military College in Surrey, was building the first electromagnets as Ohm began to publish the results of his work. And, in 1831, Michael Faraday began a series of ground-breaking experiments that led to his discovery of the principles of electromagnetic induction, described by one writer, with forgivable hyperbole, as 'the greatest experimental result ever obtained by an investigator'.

Roget's own experiments were nowhere near as significant as those of Faraday, or even of those of his old friend John Frederic Daniell, now professor at King's College, London, who invented his own improved version of the electric battery at about the same time, but he was none the less a member of the closely-connected network of scientific investigators who were pushing back the boundaries of knowledge about the still mysterious forces of electricity and magnetism. He was involved in what was, at the time, cutting edge research. In 1835, what was to prove his most influential experiment in the field led to his devising of an apparatus that is often known as Roget's Spiral. Roget's Spiral, or the Contracting Helix as it is sometimes called, demonstrates the fact that there is an attractive force between two parallel wires carrying electric current in the same direction.

Despite his immersion in work of all kinds, the years that passed after Romilly's suicide cannot have been easy for Roget and, in 1822, he had received another crushing personal blow. Alexander Marcet and he had been friends since the two men met at the Medical and Chirurgical Society more than a decade earlier. Roget was not a man who found it easy to express his emotions but it is clear from surviving correspondence that Marcet's friendship meant much to him. When the Swiss physician travelled extensively on the Continent, Roget produced a characteristically stilted but no doubt heartfelt admission that he was missing him. 'Time,' he wrote, 'has not made me less sensible of the immense void which your removal from England has left in my enjoyments.'

On 11 October 1822 Alexander Marcet, who had returned to England after his travels in Europe, died suddenly at lodgings he and his wife had taken in Great Coram Street, just around the corner from Roget's house in Bernard Street. Roget was, in fact, present at his death, although he could do nothing to save his friend, and he wrote a lengthy obituary of him. Couched in the formal prose deemed suitable for such tributes, Roget's obituary, with its references to 'the active zeal with which Marcet was animated for the advancement of knowledge and the interests of humanity' and 'the variety of talents and rectitude of judgement which marked his progress in whatever he undertook', provides little sense of personal loss. However, there can be little doubt that the death of Marcet, probably the friend to whom Roget felt closest in his life, affected him deeply.

Epidemics, Phrenology and Physiology

Throughout his life Roget was a man who was committed to the belief that science and reason were the keys to progress. Irrationality and sloppy thinking were enemies to be confronted whenever possible. Irrationality and sloppy thinking disguised as science were to be particularly condemned. It is in this context that Roget's vehement attacks in the 1820s and 1830s on phrenology or 'cranioscopy', as he often called it, can be understood. Phrenology, which originated in the ideas of an eighteenth-century Viennese physician named Franz Joseph Gall, was based on the belief that mental faculties and character traits can be gauged from the shape and size of the skull. The mind, according to phrenologists, is composed of distinct faculties and each of these faculties has a particular location in the brain. The skilled phrenologist, by examining the shape and size of the head, could determine which faculties (benevolence, self-esteem, secretiveness, spirituality etc.) were particularly marked in a patient and which were particularly lacking. Gall's ideas had been introduced to Britain by Johann Spurzheim, a German doctor born in Trier, who had published a book entitled *The Physiognomical System of Drs Gall and Spurzheim* in London in 1815 and had lectured successfully at venues throughout the country, including Roget's alma mater, Edinburgh University. Many people were sceptical of Spurzheim's claims (one anatomy teacher described phrenology as 'a piece of thorough quackery from beginning to end') but, at the time that Roget was writing, phrenology was none the less close to being a respectable science. The phrenologists themselves often made extravagant claims for their ideas. Phrenology, according to one, was 'the most intelligible and self-consistent system of mental philosophy that has ever been presented to the contemplation of inquisitive men'.

In a letter to the editor of the Britannica *Supplement*, for whom he had agreed to write an article on 'cranioscopy', Roget claimed impartiality ('I shall endeavour to give quite a fair and impartial statement of the doctrine.') but it is clear that he did not accept many of the phrenologists' claims. He did not consider their practice a legitimate science. The finished article, when it appeared, left no room to doubt Roget's own opinion. The phrenologists were no better than the silly philosophers in Jonathan Swift's satirical novel *Gulliver's Travels* who engaged in such ludicrous activities as attempting to extract sunbeams from cucumbers. 'We shall also refrain,' Roget wrote, 'from employing the weapons of ridicule against a system so vulnerable to its attacks, and which would have been so capable of affording Swift a new incident for the history of the philosophers of Laputa. The simple exposition of the sandy foundation on which it has been built, of the flimsy materials of which it has been composed, and the loose mode in which they have been put together, will suffice to enable our readers to form their own conclusions as to the soundness and solidity of the edifice.' Despite their pretensions to scientific exactness, the phrenologists were guilty of poor reasoning and fallacious logic. 'With such a convenient logic, and accommodating principles of philosophising,' Roget concluded, 'it would be easy to prove anything. We suspect, however, that on that very account, they will be rejected as having proved nothing.'

Today, although the unsubstantiated guesses of its practitioners that particular mental functions belong to particular areas of the brain have proved, by sheer chance, to be close to the truth, the inadequacy of phrenology is self-evident. This was by no means the case in the first half of the nineteenth century. It says much for the power of Roget's logical and clear-thinking intellect that he could see through the pretensions of the phrenologists to scientific knowledge of the human mind and human emotions. However, it was to lead him into a controversy which lasted for decades. For a time Roget, particularly after the publication of his scathing assessment of their practices in an article in *Encyclopaedia Britannica*, became the arch-enemy of the phrenologists. Not only did practitioners such as Andrew and George Combe, Edinburgh-based phrenologists with a talent for polemic, launch counter-attacks against the criticisms. Not only did the advocates of phrenology mount a campaign aimed at belittling Roget's scientific credentials. ('Some years ago, the name of Dr Roget would have had weight with men of science,' one wrote. 'We believe it has none at this day...') Even within the walls of his beloved Medical and Chirurgical Society, Roget faced opposition.

John Elliotson was at one time President of the society and he was one of the major figures in nineteenth-century medicine. A friend of Thackeray, who dedicated his novel *Pendennis* to him, Elliotson was one of the first British physicians to recognise the diagnostic value of the recently invented stethoscope. He was one of the first professors at the newly founded University College in London and one of the first physicians to work in the hospital that was built to provide clinical training for the medical students there. In no sense was he a quack or a practitioner on the fringes of the medical establishment. Indeed, for many years, he was at the heart of it. Yet Elliotson put his trust, not only in phrenology, but also in the equally questionable theories of mesmerism. It was he who introduced Dickens to mesmerism and the novelist famously became both a firm believer in it and and a regular practitioner of the techniques Elliotson taught him. A founder of the Phrenological Society of London in 1823, Elliotson published widely on both phrenology and mesmerism. His 1843 book, *Surgical Operations in the Mesmeric State without Pain*, as its title implies, advocated the use of mesmerism in even the most challenging of cases.

With advocates of this stature, phrenology was no easy target for Roget's scorn. In the middle decades of the nineteenth century, it had its adherents everywhere from university colleges to royal palaces (in 1841 George Combe was invited to examine the head of the infant Prince of Wales and report what the bumps on it suggested about his burgeoning character) but Roget persisted in his view that it was illogical and unscientific. His essay in the seventh edition of *Encyclopaedia Britannica* was one of the most significant of all the attacks made on phrenology at the time, largely because of the characteristic thoroughness and clarity with which Roget marshalled his evidence and his arguments. He spent much time reading and assessing the work of phrenologists and he even chose to examine the skulls and casts in a famous collection made by a London phrenologist named De Ville. His conclusion – that the phrenologists' writings did not make consistent and logical sense and that the skulls in De Ville's collection provided little evidence to prove Gall's and Spurzheim's theories – was unequivocal. He gently mocked the suggestion by some advocates of phrenology that they formed a persecuted minority of advanced thinkers. 'When we consider,' he wrote, 'that the present age is not one in which there is any lack of credulity, or in which a doctrine is likely to be repudiated on the score of its novelty or extravagance, we cannot but smile at the complaints of persecution uttered by the votaries of the system of Dr Gall, and at the attempts they make to set up a parallel between its reception in this country, in these times, and that which, two centuries ago, attended the speculations of Galileo, and subjected him to the tyrannous cognisance of the

Inquisition; or to establish an analogy between the dogmas of phrenology and the discoveries of the circulation of blood, and of the analysis of light, which have immortalised the names of Harvey and of Newton.'

Roget's belief was the same as it had always been. Phrenology was not a science. Yet it would not go away. Its popularity continued throughout much of the nineteenth century, despite the paper wars between the phrenologists on one side and their critics, of whom Roget was one of the most important, on the other. George Combe's 1828 book, *The Constitution of Man*, was one of the 'scientific' bestsellers of its time, selling more than twice as many copies in its first thirty years of publication as Charles Darwin's infinitely more valuable work, *The Origin of Species*, did in the thirty years after its first appearance in 1859.

Attacks on the phrenologists took up only a small proportion of Roget's time. He was as busy as he always was in a dozen different fields. The antidote to the personal losses he had suffered continued to be work. Just before Marcet's death Roget had written to his friend, implying that he was tired and out of sorts. 'I am indeed grown rather weary of forming projects,' he remarked, 'having become less sanguine as to the power of realising them.' However, the evidence suggests that Roget was as active as ever. His own medical practice and his work at the Northern Dispensary continued. So too did his private research into the innumerable subjects that fascinated him. He was still playing a leading role in the affairs of half a dozen scientific societies. In 1822 and 1823 he gave a series of well-received lectures at the Royal Institution on a range of scientific subjects from 'The Function of the Skeleton' to 'Introduction to Perception and Feelings in Animals'. And, in 1823, he was faced by one of the most puzzling and demanding cases of his medical career – an epidemic among prisoners at the Millbank Penitentiary.

Occupying ground now covered by Tate Britain, Millbank Penitentiary was originally the brainchild of Roget's brief collaborator on the ill-fated Frigidarium, Jeremy Bentham. Bentham had outlined his plan for a revolutionary new form of prison (prisoners occupying the circumference of a circular building under perpetual surveillance by warders in the centre) in a work of 1791 entitled *The Panopticon*. He invested his own money in the project and lost most of it when the scheme foundered. The government of George III took over and completed the building but not to Bentham's original plans. The philosopher was repaid much of the money he had lost, although he remained bitter about the way he had been treated as the title of the pamphlet he wrote on the dispute makes clear. *History of the War between Jeremy Bentham and George the Third, by One of the Belligerents* remained unpublished in Bentham's lifetime but reveals just how much the failure of his more ambitious plans for the Panopticon rankled.

In February 1823, Roget and another physician, Peter Mere Latham. were called in to the prison to investigate a disease amongst its inmates that was threatening to spiral out of control. Increasing numbers of the prisoners, both male and female, were being confined to the infirmary, suffering from violent diarrhoea and vomiting. Several had died. Amid growing concerns that Millbank, supposedly an ideal and progressive institution, was proving no better at safeguarding the health of its inmates than the old jails like Newgate, Roget and Latham were given the delicate task of looking in to what was happening.

Latham was ten years younger than Roget and was presumably, to a large extent, the junior partner in the investigative team but he was to go on to a distinguished career, becoming both Physician Extraordinary to Queen Victoria and an early specialist in heart disease. Three months later, the two men made their first report, suggesting that the problem was a kind of scurvy caused by inadequacies in the diet. A change of diet had already been instituted and it was believed that the epidemic had been brought under control. However, by the time Roget's and Latham's first report was published, their original optimism that they had brought the epidemic under control was looking premature. The disease, whatever it was, had once again taken over the prison. Indeed on 5 April, the very day that the report was published, 448 out of 858 prisoners were sick. Roget's and Latham's optimistic conclusion that there was 'now no obstacle to the entire re-establishment of the healthy state of the Penitentiary' was made to look more than a little foolish. By the summer thirty prisoners had died and nearly all the prisoners in Millbank had at least some of the symptoms, most notably and unpleasantly uncontrollable diarrhoea. The epidemic was fast becoming not only a killer within the walls of the prison but a potential scandal outside them. Newspapers and MPs alike were calling for a solution. A select committee of the House of Commons was appointed to investigate the epidemic and the handling of it. Controversies of all kinds began to rage. Earlier in the course of the investigation, one of the medical officers at the prison, a fellow member with Roget of the Medical and Chirurgical Society named Hutchinson, had been dismissed. There is a delicate suggestion in his dismissal letter that Hutchinson was over-fond of drink. 'The directions which you give in cases which come under your consideration after dinner,' the letter euphemistically stated, 'are marked with haste and precipitation, which are not observable in an earlier part of the day.' Hutchinson was not slow to respond to the slur on his character and he issued pamphlets defending his actions and his reputation. The parliamentary committee, when it reported, found largely in favour of Roget and Latham and the mercury treatment they eventually used on the sick prisoners.

Yet, despite all that the physicians did, the disease continued to rage on. Eventually, Roget and Latham were reduced to what might well seem the rather desperate expedient of suggesting that all the prisoners should be given pardons since, when they were all packed into the prison together, they continued to re-infect one another. Despite criticism in the press, this was indeed what was done with many of the women prisoners and, in April 1824, an Act of Parliament was passed, promoted by the then Home Secretary Sir Robert Peel, which gave the authorities the power to distribute male prisoners throughout the hulks lying along the Thames and thus reduce the overcrowding in Millbank.

After fifteen months, Roget's largely unsuccessful attempts to alleviate the suffering of the prisoners were over. The Millbank epidemic, at first sight, may not appear to have been his finest hour. Roget himself may well have assumed this. Although Latham went on to publish a self-exculpatory pamphlet entitled *An Account of the Disease lately prevalent at the General Penitentiary*, his older and more experienced colleague kept his thoughts largely to himself. Yet there is another perspective on it that gives Roget greater credit. His biographer, DL Emblen, argues that, at times during the investigation, he and Latham were tantalisingly close to enunciating the germ theory of disease, especially in the statement that 'some injurious influence has been in operation over and above the causes to which the epidemic was originally imputed... If it consist of contagion (and such possibly may be the case), dysentery will still probably linger in the prison as long as any remain there who have not suffered it; and then, due to the place, to the season, or to the moral and physical condition of the people so confined, it may be still capable of renewing the same disease, or of creating another form of epidemic.' The germ theory of disease was not to be properly proposed until Louis Pasteur did so in the 1860s but Emblen claims that here the two men were groping towards an understanding of the epidemic that stepped beyond the boundaries of ideas current at the time.

There are difficulties with this line of argument. Why, for example, if Roget and Latham thought that the disease was contagious, did they recommend transferring the prisoners elsewhere? Why did Roget, who had experience of contagious diseases dating back to his time in Manchester and his association with John Ferriar, not recognise the problem more swiftly? And vague talk of 'some injurious influence' is a long way away from any real understanding of the kind of theory Pasteur was to expound. Yet there is an element of truth in Emblen's claim. The two doctors did glimpse the possibility of a new theory to explain the transmission of a disease from one person to another but, caught up in the practical problems they faced during the epidemic and with no knowledge of what the agents of transmission could possibly be, they were unable to follow up on their glimpsed insights.

This was not to be the last time that Roget was involved in a government-sponsored enquiry that not only proved difficult to manage, but also led him towards the brink of a major scientific breakthrough. In 1828, he was appointed, by a special commission of George IV, to undertake a pioneering investigation into the state of London's water. Together with William Thomas Brande, a former Professor of Chemistry at the Royal Institution, and Thomas Telford, the famous engineer of roads and bridges after whom Telford New Town in Shropshire is named, Roget was given the opportunity to study how effective and how hygienic the water supply was. At the time the supply of water to the capital's households was in the hands of a range of private companies, all competing with one another and, in most cases, drawing their water from the deeply polluted Thames. The dangers of a water supply based on a river which was also, in effect, the city's main drain were clear enough but, in an age when government intervention in such matters was deemed both impractical and undesirable, any investigation into it was bound to be compromised. Even before they started their investigation, Roget and his colleagues had been given clear boundaries beyond which they were not supposed to trespass. Their report was supposed to be merely descriptive of the current situation and was to include no recommendations for future actions. (In the event, they managed to smuggle what they called 'plans of remedies', including ideas for a primitive filter to purify the Thames water, into the finished report but these were largely ignored.)

The conclusions that Roget, Brande and Telford reached now seem bland to the point of uselessness. 'We are of opinion,' they wrote, 'that the present state of the supply of Water to the Metropolis is susceptible of and requires improvement; that many of the complaints respecting the quality of the Water are well founded, and that it ought to be derived from other sources than those now resorted to, and guarded by such restrictions as shall at all times ensure its cleanliness and purity.' Yet, given the restrictions imposed on them from the start, it is difficult to see what more they could have done.

One of the primary dangers of the water supply in London at the time of Roget's report was cholera, a water-borne disease which produced appalling symptoms of diarrhoea and vomiting and often ended for sufferers in a grim and revolting death. That the report by Roget and his colleagues proved of little practical use is demonstrated by the fact that one of the most serious outbreaks of cholera in the capital took place only a few short years after it was issued. In 1832 the disease struck the East End of London, causing thousands of deaths. However, in retrospect, the 1828 report can be seen as one of the first real acknowledgements of the problem of London's water supply and the decades that followed saw an increasing awareness that the capital's drinking water was a dangerous commodity. It was left to the Yorkshire physician, John Snow, working in London during a later cholera epidemic in the 1850s, to prove conclusively that there was a link between the disease and the water supply and to show how it was transmitted. There is a pleasing historical coincidence in the fact that Snow's ground-breaking investigation focused on a water pump in Broad Street, the street where Roget was born.

During all this period of intense and demanding work, Roget's relationships with his closest family proved fraught with difficulties. In the aftermath of the suicide of her brother, Catherine Roget's own mental health steadily deteriorated. A proposal that Samuel Romilly's close friend and literary executor, John Whishaw, should publish the dead man's journals caused her and her daughter great anxiety that private family matters would become public. Annette wrote to her brother, asking for his help in quashing the idea. 'I cannot conceive that a man has the right to speak of living persons in any publication if these people object to being mentioned,' she told him. 'It is well known that one cannot do this with honour.' Not for the first time in their correspondence, Annette sounded nearly hysterical, claiming that, 'I will certainly withdraw from all society if you are not able to succeed with Mr Whishaw'.

The idea was eventually dropped but, as the years passed, Catherine Roget's mental well-being did not improve. She became liable to attacks of both paranoia, in which she believed that servants and even family friends were conspiring to thwart her wishes and to do her harm, and amnesia, in which memories of the events in her life either disappeared or were re-worked into new personal narratives of her past. Meanwhile Annette was rapidly descending into embittered spinsterhood, deeply resentful of the fate that had forced her into the responsibility of looking after her increasingly troublesome mother. In 1820, the two women moved out of Bernard Street and London and back to Ilfracombe, one of the succession of resort towns in which they had lived in earlier days. It was a place that Annette had little reason to remember with affection and, from it, she sent letters back to her brother which would read as almost comically gloomy and self-pitying if it were not for the fact that they clearly reflected a deep unhappiness. 'If only the future could present anything agreeable to me, but since there is nothing ahead but misery, I often hope that the sore foot I have would be fatal. The picture that I have in front of me – to live always, for the rest of my miserable life, in furnished apartments in this place worries me so much that I lose all appetite and all repose.' Even the food in Ilfracombe, when she could face it, added to her miseries. 'I cannot accustom myself to the common black bread, the stinking butter, and the horrible beer here, and my stomach has become so delicate that I exist almost entirely on plum pudding and potatoes.'

For more than a decade, looking after Catherine Roget became an increasingly hard burden for her daughter to bear. Reading the letters Annette wrote to her brother, it is difficult to avoid the conclusion that their mother was suffering from some kind of senile dementia. In one letter, written after returning to Ilfracombe from a visit to Bernard Street, Annette is clearly close to despair. 'It is then that my mother is absolutely unmanageable, for it is then that she runs upstairs and looks in the bedrooms to see if she has left anything in the drawers. It is in vain that I tell her that we have only entered the place for a few moments... I always fear that she is going to burst out in front of everyone with the extraordinary ideas that have come into her head. I have never been able to make her understand that we have left London and are travelling to Ilfracombe. For several mornings after our arrival, she was packing her things to travel again, and what is more remarkable, at the end of two days only, she thought we had already dwelt in Ilfracombe for several months.'

Roget was clearly very fond of his sister but, reading the letters of advice he wrote to her over the years, it seems clear that he failed almost completely to understand and appreciate the frustrations of an intelligent and sensitive woman who was denied any real means of expressing either her feelings or her intelligence. Her exasperated response to one letter, in which her well-meaning but obtuse brother had been suggesting that she would benefit from the liberty she would gain if their mother was placed in a rest-home, speaks volumes: 'Tell me clearly what kind of life I ought in that case to lead, and if this liberty, of which you speak, means any more than to live in furnished apartments in one place and another... The only liberty that I desire is simply that of being able to calm my mind with peaceful studies, some agreeable daily occupations joined certainly to some household duties.' In the circumstances in which she was obliged to live, there was little chance that Annette could achieve even this simple desire.

However, it was also during this period, when his mother and sister were descending further and further into depression and despondency, that Roget himself found a new source of personal happiness. On 18 November 1824, aged forty-five, he married. There is little earlier evidence of Roget's emotional life and of his relationships with women beyond the often complex ones with his mother and sister. For a number of years before and after 1820, Jane Griffin, later to become the wife of the celebrated explorer Sir John Franklin, seems to have set her cap at him. Jane, the daughter of a wealthy London merchant, again of Huguenot stock, was to prove her formidable determination and powers of persuasion in later decades when, as Lady Franklin, she steamrollered the Admiralty into sending out numerous expeditions in search of her husband, lost in the Arctic during a misconceived attempt to discover the Northwest Passage. Her attempts to manoeuvre Roget into marriage proved less successful.

The two met for the first time in 1809, probably through mutual acquaintances in the capital's Huguenot community, but it was not until nearly a decade later that the doctor, approaching forty, and the merchant's daughter, entering her late twenties and in danger of being trapped in an unwanted spinsterhood, began to grow closer. Jane Griffin went to see Roget lecture at the Royal Institution. Roget joined a Book Society that Jane and her younger sister had organised. Friends of both of them began to speak of a possible marriage. Jane, sounding more girlishly coy than any clever and resourceful woman approaching thirty should probably do, confided her thoughts about 'the individual whose name I dare not write' to her journal. The unnamed Roget was, she thought, 'superior to most men' and 'incapable of any thing inconsistent with the goodness of his heart and the rectitude of his principles'. In a slow and formal dance of courtship, the two seemed to be moving towards matrimony. It was not to be. Although Roget was undoubtedly attracted to Jane's high intelligence and strong personality, he refused to commit himself. He may well have been wary of a woman so clearly determined to have her own way. As Sir John Franklin was to discover, what Jane wanted, Jane almost invariably got. To a middle-aged bachelor like Roget, accustomed to the regular routines of work he had created, such single-mindedness probably seemed a threat. After several years of inconclusive friendship, the affair, such as it was, came to an end in slightly mystifying circumstances when Jane decided that Roget, no longer so superior to other men, had been guilty of an unforgiveable breach of manners and etiquette.

To most of his acquaintances, Roget may well have seemed one of nature's bachelors and many may have been surprised by his marriage. His bride was Mary Taylor Hobson, sixteen years younger than her husband and the only daughter of a wealthy cotton merchant from Liverpool named Jonathan Hobson. Liverpool was a place with which Roget had long had connections. He had visited the city during his years in Manchester. One of his closest friends from the Medical and Chirurgical Society, John Bostock, worked for a number of years in the infirmary there. Etienne Dumont had stayed in the city and knew the Hobson family. When Roget's marriage plans were announced, Dumont wrote to his protégé, recalling earlier meetings with Mary. 'No idea of your plans occurred to me then, but I noticed in your young friend an ease and a grace which are not very common, even in the most likeable persons of her age.'

Congratulations on his marriage, which took place at the parish church of St Philip in Liverpool, reached Roget from all sides – from colleagues in the innumerable scientific and intellectual societies of which he was a member to old friends like Lovell Edgeworth, long released from his French prison and now in Ireland, struggling to return the family estates to some kind of prosperity. Annette wrote, rather stiffly, from Ilfracombe to her new sister-in-law but included in her letter a poignant admission of, 'How often have I wished for a sister who could share with me, and lighten my difficulties, and who could convert a melancholy and fatiguing tête-à-tête into a cheerful fireside!' She also acknowledged in the same letter how far Catherine Roget was from an awareness of what was happening in the lives of others. 'I omit the ceremony of sending my Mother's regards – my Brother knows how impossible it is to impress on her mind the event which has given her a daughter-in-law.' When Mary gave birth in 1825, Catherine still had little idea of who she was and, informed of the happy event by her daughter, kept asking, 'Who is she?'

On 9 December 1824, less than a month after his marriage, Roget read one of the most important of all his papers to the Royal Society. 'Explanation of an Optical

Deception in the Appearance of the Spokes of a Wheel Seen Through Vertical Apertures' may have an exceedingly cumbersome title but its publication marked one of the most important moments in the prehistory of the cinema. Roget had long been fascinated by optical phenomena. In 1816, the invention of the kaleidoscope by the Scottish scientist David Brewster had caught his attention. He was not alone in this – the kaleidoscope became one of the passing sensations of the Regency era and hundreds of thousands were manufactured and sold – but it was typical of Roget that he should feel compelled to investigate the subject more deeply. He wrote an article on kaleidoscopes for *Blackwood's Magazine* in 1818, in which he not only praised Brewster, claiming that, 'In the memory of man, no invention, and no work, whether addressed to the imagination or to the understanding, ever produced such an effect', but also suggested improvements to the design of the instrument. In 1824, when the *Encyclopaedia Britannica* required an article on kaleidoscopes, it was Roget who supplied it.

The paper presented to the Royal Society in the same year described another optical phenomenon – his own experience of the strange effects he had noticed when looking through venetian blinds at the traffic passing by in Bernard Street. (He was sufficiently intrigued by them to employ a street vendor to move his cart up and down the street and past the window in order to reproduce deliberately the movement he had first observed accidentally.)

'A curious optical deception takes place when a

carriage wheel, rolling along the ground, is viewed through the intervals of a series of vertical bars, such as those of a palisade or of a Venetian blind. Under these circumstances the spokes of the wheel, instead of appearing straight, as they would naturally do if no bars intervened, seem to have a considerable degree of curvature.'

This may seem like a very trivial observation on which to build a paper presented to the Royal Society, the nation's oldest and most prestigious scientific society, but it is to Roget's credit that he immediately recognised the importance of what he had seen. He realised that what was happening was that the slats on the Venetian blinds were acting to divide his vision of the motion into individual frames and that it was this that was causing the distortion. He was able to take his deductions one step further. He saw links between what he had seen from his Bernard Street window and other visual phenomena.

'The true principle, then, on which this phenomenon depends is the same as that to which is referable the illusion that occurs when a bright object is wheeled rapidly round in a circle, giving rise to the appearance of a line of light throughout the whole circumference; namely, that an impression made by a pencil of rays on the retina, if sufficiently vivid, will remain for a certain time after the cause has ceased.'

Although critics have pointed out that, despite claims to the contrary that regularly appear in histories of cinema's precursors, he never actually used the phrase, it is none the less clear from this quotation that Roget had understood the phenomenon of 'persistence of vision' on which motion pictures are based. Persistence of vision can be defined as the perceptual process by which the brain or the retina retains an image for a brief split second after the image has, in reality, disappeared. Thus it is also the means by which we see movies as motion rather than simply a succession of individual, unmoving frames of film. Some psychologists now deny the scientific validity of the ideas behind persistence of vision but, using the definition accepted for so long, Roget undoubtedly deserves the credit he has been given for describing an effect to which no one had given much thought before and for recognising its general application to the ways in which we see.

The phenomenon Roget had described stimulated the inquiring mind of one of the greatest scientists of the age. Michael Faraday, pioneer in electrical research, was a professor at the Royal Institution and it was there, in December 1830, that he gave a lecture, published a couple of months later, entitled 'On a Peculiar Class of Optical Deceptions'. Faraday had been intrigued by Roget's descriptions and analysis of the way the spokes of the carriage wheel appeared when viewed through the slats of the blind and linked it with his own observations of two sets of cogwheels rotating in opposite directions. Whenever the cogwheels aligned, 'there was immediately the distinct, though shadowy resemblance of cogs moving slowly in one direction'. In his paper, Faraday went to write that, 'the eye has the power, as is well known, of retaining visual impressions for a sensible period of time;

and in this way, recurring actions, made sufficiently near to each other, are perceptibly connected, and made to appear as a continuous impression'. He even had a series of discs specially made for him in order to investigate the phenomenon in the comfort of his own study.

One of the other consequences of the growing understanding of the phenomenon following Roget's pioneering paper, and Faraday's subsequent investigations into it, was a surge in the production of toys and mechanical devices in the 1830s which made use of it. Joseph Plateau, for example, was a Belgian physicist and mathematician who had long been interested in visual perception and the impression of light and colour on the eye. He knew of Faraday's work (which had been translated and published abroad) and, in 1833, he produced what he called a Phenakistoscope. This consisted of two discs, one with a sequence of images around its circumference and the other with a number of equidistant slits on it through which a viewer could look. When the discs were spun at the right speed, the images appeared to move. Independently of Plateau, an Austrian named Simon von Stampfer who had also read Faraday's work, invented a very similar device which made use of the phenomena Roget and Faraday had described to produce the illusion of motion. It came to be known as a Stroboscope.

According to Roget, he had actually pre-empted Plateau and Stampfer and had invented a machine very like theirs before they had done but he had done nothing to publicise or market it. In 1834, he claimed that

Faraday's paper had rekindled his own interest in optical phenomena and this 'led me to the invention of the instrument which has since been introduced into notice under the name of the Phantasmascope or Phenakistoscope. I constructed several of these at that period (in the spring of 1831) which I showed to my friends; but in consequence of occupations and cares of a more serious kind, I did not publish any account of this invention, which was reproduced on the continent in the year 1833.'

Whoever really was the first to invent the device is almost immaterial. Plateau's Phenakistoscope, Stampfer's Stroboscope and Roget's mysterious and unnamed instrument stand at the beginning of a line which leads directly, via dozens of other optical toys of the nineteenth century (the Zoetrope, the Praxinoscope, the Electrotachyscope), to the invention of motion pictures. As one cinema historian put it more than fifty years ago, 'Once Roget enunciated his theory… the advance toward motion pictures and motion picture projection was rapid and direct. Almost immediately scientists throughout Europe began putting his theory to the test. Their devices may have resembled children's toys – whirling discs, twirling coins, booklets of pictures flipped with the thumb – but they quickly established the basic truth of Roget's contention that through some peculiarity of the eye an image is retained for a fraction of a second longer than it actually appears. On this peculiarity rests the fortune of the entire motion picture industry.'

All the evidence we have, from letters both by and to

the Rogets and from such chance survivals as the brief
journals that Mary Roget kept at various times, suggests
that their marriage was a loving and successful one. There
were two children. On 27 October 1825, a daughter,
Catherine Mary Roget, was born and a son, John Lewis
Roget, destined to continue his father's work on the
Thesaurus, followed on 28 April 1828. In 1830, the
Rogets crossed the Channel and travelled to Paris, a
journey recorded by Mary in one of the journals she kept
intermittently throughout her married life. Mary Roget's
impressions of France were at first not much more
favourable than her husband's had been thirty years
earlier. At Le Havre she was distressed by a woman in the
customs house who 'proceeded to examine my person,
which she did very ineffectually, and I might have been
spared the annoyance of having her hand inserted underneath my stays'. Things got no better when they were
taken to their lodgings. 'We soon walked to the inn, and
were immediately shown to our room. But the dismay of
an English lady was considerable to find that this room
was but a step raised above the courtyard, a tiled floor
without carpet and two very high windows, with very thin
muslin curtains half-way up, opening into the court or
public entrance, so that it was exactly like sleeping in the
street. I did not like the idea of undressing in so exposed
a situation.'

However, as the days passed, Mary began to enjoy her
first experiences of a foreign country rather more. A
sailing trip up the Seine was 'very enchanting' and 'as we

approached Rouen the hills began to diminish in height, and the magnificent cathedral soon towered above every other object'. Mary began to enjoy the trip. 'The first appearance of the town, with the heights of St. Catherine behind, is magnificent,' she wrote. 'The boulevards afford trees, which appear to mingle with the shipping. The evening sun was shining upon the town and the picture was quite enchanting.' Two weeks in Paris, with all the sights to see and the entertainments to attend, completed Mary's conversion into more of a Francophile than her husband, with his memories of Napoleonic threats several decades earlier, would ever be.

On their return to England, unfortunately, a dark cloud was soon to appear on the horizon of the Rogets' marriage and to grow in size over a number of years. Throughout the early 1830s, Mary suffered increasingly from a painful illness. From the evidence of Roget's letters to friends and family, it seems to have been some kind of cancer. In a letter of August 1832 to Mary's brother Sam, Roget wrote that, 'The tumour continues to enlarge and what is still more distressing, is giving her a constant feeling of uneasiness and often of pain. She walks with greater difficulty, and is now quite unable to bear the shaking of a carriage... The future is to me all mist and darkness through which I cannot yet see my way. My poor children, too – what will become of them! I know it is my duty to be patient and to submit, but the task is hard. I trust I may have sufficient fortitude to go through with it.' All efforts to halt the progress of the illness proved futile and, throughout the winter of 1832 and the spring of 1833, she continued to suffer from its painful symptoms. She, and her family, were obliged to face the truth that she was not going to get better.

On 12 April 1833, Mary Roget finally died at the age of only thirty-eight. Roget, utterly distraught, was looked after by the Hobson family in Liverpool over the summer. Unsurprisingly, as a man who had found emotional happiness late in life, only to have it cruelly snatched away from him, he was prostrated by grief and his recovery from his bereavement was a slow one. It was autumn before he returned to London and Bernard Street. There further distress awaited him as he was obliged to sort through Mary's belongings. Locked in her desk, he found a letter, written at some point in her prolonged illness, which must have made almost unbearably poignant reading for him: 'These few lines will be seen by you alone. They are to repeat to you, my precious, how dearly I love you, and to thank you for the sweet tenderness and kindness which have made the last year of my life so very very happy. Do not, love, think of me in sorrow for God will let us be happy again where we need not fear to be separated any more.' It was signed 'My ever precious friend, my darling husband, your Mary Roget'.

Roget and the Royal Society

As we have seen, Roget had become a Fellow of the Royal Society, able to place the three important letters 'FRS' after his name, in 1815 but his involvement with the Society most certainly did not stop there. Both during the years of his marriage and his decades as a widower, he continued to make major contributions to its work. In 1827, three years after his marriage, he was elected its Secretary, a position he was eventually to hold for more than two decades. This made Roget one of the most powerful figures in British scientific life at the time and led to various recognitions of his standing from honorary memberships in other societies to the naming of a Cape in Antarctica after him. (Cape Roget, first named by the polar explorer John Ross, still features on maps of the continent.) However, it certainly did not render him immune from criticism. His long tenure as Secretary coincided with a series of attacks on the Royal Society which embodied one of the great schisms in nineteenth-century science. In the early decades of the Victorian era there was a growing tension between the long-established amateurism (often in the best sense of the word) of gentlemen interested in what was still called 'natural philosophy' and the professionalism increasingly demanded by more cutting-edge practitioners of science.

One of the most persistent of the Society's critics was Charles Babbage who once described its council as 'a collection of men who elect each other to office and then dine together, at the expense of this society, to praise each other over wine and give each other medals'. Babbage, born in Walworth, London in 1791, was one of the greatest British mathematicians of the nineteenth century and a man far ahead of his time. He spent nearly half a century working on mechanical calculating machines (an early version called the Difference Engine and a later model known as the Analytical Engine) which anticipated many of the ideas, if not the technology, in electronic computing of the last fifty years. Today, Babbage is remembered almost exclusively as a computer pioneer but he was a man of many accomplishments in subjects as different as cryptography and natural theology. He was also a man of some eccentricity, obsessed by the accumulation and analysis of precise data in all areas, irrespective of any practical application the results might have. Babbage once published in *Mechanics' Magazine* a 'Table of the Relative Frequency of the Causes of Breaking of Plate Glass Windows', detailing 464 breakages, of which 'drunken men, women, or boys' were responsible for 14. Babbage himself believed the table would be 'of value in many respects', but it is difficult to see what benefit readers of the magazine could have had from it. A stickler for accuracy, he was distressed by Lord Tennyson's cavalier use of statistics in a poem entitled *The Vision of Sin* where the poet had written the lines, 'Every moment dies a man/Every moment one is born.' Babbage wrote to Tennyson to correct his error: 'I need hardly point out to you that this calculation would tend to keep the sum total of the world's population in a state of perpetual equipoise, whereas it is a well-known fact that the said sum total is constantly on the increase. I would therefore take the liberty of suggesting that in the next edition of your excellent poem the erroneous calculation to which I refer should be corrected as follows: "Every moment dies a man/And one and a sixteenth is born." I may add that the exact figures are 1.067 but something must, of course, be conceded to the laws of metre.'

This was the strange and visionary scientific and mathematical genius who was to become a regular thorn in Roget's side over the years. In 1828, Babbage was appointed to a committee that the officers of the Society reluctantly established to look into possible reforms but, when it appeared, the committee's report was shelved and ignored. Babbage was understandably furious. Two years later, he published a book entitled *Reflections on the Decline of Science in England* in which he claimed that the country was falling behind rivals like France and Germany in the promotion of science and that the Royal Society, hidebound by amateurism and fusty tradition, bore much of the responsibility for this. He analysed the membership of the Society, pointing out how few members had produced genuinely significant scientific work and argued, in effect, that the Society had become more a self-serving and inward-looking clique than a real and progressive scientific body. Roget had had a long and apparently amiable acquaintance with Babbage, whose work on automatic calculating machines was fascinating to a man who had himself created an improved version of the slide rule. He even provided what amounted to a laudatory reference for the younger man when he was seeking a professorship at Edinburgh. None the less Babbage singled Roget out for particular criticism, accusing him of irregularities in the keeping of the Society's records that were designed to cover up quite justified dissatisfaction with the way the Society was run.

Roget responded immediately to Babbage's accusations of dishonest behaviour. Babbage had, Roget thought, 'spent an immense time in ransacking the records of the Society with an industry worthy of a better cause' but his claims were erroneous and based on misunderstandings and misinformation. The stage, however, was set for a long and often rancorous debate between those, like Roget, who defended the status quo, and those, like Babbage, who demanded reform. In a flurry of accusation and counter-accusation, letters were written to *The Times*, pamphlets were published and clamorous meetings were held in which argument raged. The astronomer Sir James South, famous for his work with John Herschel in cataloguing stars, was one of the boldest and most outspoken of the Society's critics, publishing a short pamphlet entitled *Charges Against the President and Councils of the Royal*

Society in which he outlined a series of alleged 'crimes' which ranged from misuse of the Society's funds to the awarding of Society medals to undeserving recipients. Perhaps unsurprisingly, Roget and his fellow officers refused to accept a copy of the pamphlet when South cheekily offered to donate one to the Society's library but, to the reformers, this was just another sign of closed minds in high office.

The Society elections of 1830 provided the opportunity for a battle between the old guard and the would-be reformers. The President, first chosen in 1827, was a Cornish landowner and MP named Davies Gilbert, an early patron of Humphry Davy, who was known as much for his antiquarian interest in his county's history and folklore as he was for his scientific achievements. Although he had proved a strong parliamentary advocate of the importance of science and scientific ventures, he was not by anyone's reckoning, including his own, an innovative or significant practitioner of science himself. When Gilbert announced that he would not be putting himself forward for re-election the reformers proposed John Herschel, South's partner in the compilation of data about the stars and a friend of Babbage since their undergraduate days at Cambridge, as President. Herschel was not eager for the honour. He wrote to Babbage, claiming that, 'I love science too well to be very easily induced to throw away the small part of the one lifetime I have to bestow it on the affairs of a public body which has proved to be... a continued source of dispute and annoyance.' Babbage, however, was insistent, and Herschel eventually agreed to stand. Gilbert and Roget and the other officers of the Society wanted the Duke of Sussex, the sixth son of George III, to take over the presidency. The Duke, of course, had no scientific credentials worth mentioning in the same breath as those of Herschel but the social cachet of having a Royal Duke as President was considerable. After much manoeuvring and in-fighting, the Duke won the election by 119 votes to 111 and the status quo was maintained.

The reformers were confirmed in their belief that the Royal Society was a home for scientific dinosaurs and many of them, including Babbage, were instrumental in the founding in 1831 of the British Association for the Advancement of Science. The prime mover in the new association was actually David Brewster, the Scottish scientist and inventor of the kaleidoscope whom Roget so admired, but many of its stated aims owed much to the concerns expressed by Babbage in *Reflections on the Decline of Science in England*. In his own writings, Brewster had also shown anxiety about the future of science in England. The country, he thought, was in danger of losing the pre-eminence it had once had: (England's) 'machinery has been exported to distant markets; the inventions of her philosophers, slighted at home, have been eagerly introduced abroad; her scientific institutions have been discouraged and even abolished; the articles which she supplied to other states have been gradually manufactured by themselves; and, one after another, many of the best arts of England have been transferred to other nations.'

These are worries that seem perennial in the scientific community – they carry echoes of future concerns about the 'brain drain' in the 1950s and 1960s or the deteriorating quality of scientific education in the twenty-first century – but they were undoubtedly genuine and, to some extent, justified.

Immediately after the first meeting of the British Association for the Advancement of Science, which took place in York on 26 September, its objects were explicitly stated. They were 'to give a stronger impulse and more systematic direction to scientific inquiry, to obtain a greater degree of national attention to the objects of science, and a removal of those disadvantages which impede its progress, and to promote the intercourse of the cultivators of science with one another, and with foreign philosophers'. Given a few changes in the nineteenth-century language, these are aims to which most members of the Association today could give assent. (That the battle lines between old and new were not as clearly defined in 1831 as might sometimes appear is indicated by the fact that Roget was himself an early member of the British Association.)

Yet it was also during the years of intense pressure created by his work for the Royal Society that Roget produced the book for which he (and probably most of his contemporaries) believed that he would be remembered by posterity. *Animal and Vegetable Physiology Considered with Reference to Natural Theology* appeared in 1834. It was a work that cost him much to write. In the preface he acknowledged that it had been accompanied by 'long protracted anxieties and afflictions, and by the almost overwhelming pressure of domestic calamity', a clear reference to the loss of his wife. The book was published as one of the so-called Bridgewater Treatises. The Earl of Bridgewater was an aristocrat and scholar who was known for such eccentricities as giving dinner parties for his dogs at which the canine diners were carefully dressed in the finest fashions of the day. When he died in 1829 he not only bequeathed a collection of highly valuable manuscripts to the British Museum but he also left money for the publication of a major work to illustrate 'the Power, Wisdom and Goodness of God as manifested in the Creation'. Eventually his executors decided that the Earl's wish could not be fulfilled in a single volume and a series of books, including the one by Roget, was commissioned.

Other treatises were written by leading lights in the scientific community of the time. William Whewell, a carpenter's son from Lancaster who had become a Cambridge professor, wrote on astronomy and physics; Charles Bell, a Scottish anatomist who had been connected with the Great Windmill School of Medicine in the years when Roget had lectured there, produced the most esoteric of the treatises in *The Hand: Its Mechanism and Vital Endowments as Evincing Design*; William Prout, a chemist and physician, examined an unlikely combination of subjects in *Chemistry, Meteorology, and the Function of Digestion, considered with reference to Natural Theology*; the geologist and palaeontologist William Buckland surveyed his own particular subjects in search of God's handiwork. (As well as being a major scientist, Buckland was also, like the Earl, an exceedingly eccentric man in an age of eccentrics. One of his stated aims in life was to eat his way through the animal kingdom, tasting the flesh of as many creatures as he could. Hedgehog, alligator, ostrich and sea slug all appeared on the menu at his dinner parties and one of his favourite dishes was toasted mice. He confessed that the two nastiest of all his culinary experiences had been snacking on bluebottles and tucking in to moles. According to another story, Buckland once visited a cathedral in Italy where the blood of a saint was said to be always fresh on the floor of a chapel, never evaporating or vanishing. The scientist tasted the 'blood' and was able to state confidently from previous experience that it was, in fact, bats' urine.)

As Roget explained in his characteristically ponderous prose, he wanted his Bridgewater Treatise to be 'a useful introduction to the study of Natural History; the pursuit of which will be found not only to supply inexhaustible sources of intellectual gratification, but also to furnish, to contemplative minds, a rich fountain of religious instruction'. Viewed with the hindsight of posterity, the irony is that Roget's treatise, and the others for which the Earl's bequest paid, appeared at a time when science and scientific discovery were working more to undermine the tenets of revealed religion than to support them. It was not just that, for example, it was becoming more and more difficult to reconcile Biblical time with the story that geologists were unearthing from the rocks. That was inconvenient for conventionally-minded natural theologians but it did not present an insuperable problem. It was more that the entire 'argument by design' – the assumption that the order and complexity of the universe necessarily implied a divine creator – was under threat in the middle decades of the nineteenth century.

The Bridgewater Treatises looked backwards to a tradition exemplified by William Paley's influential book *Natural Theology or Evidences of the Existence and Attributes of the Deity*, first published in 1802, which Roget had certainly read and studied soon after it appeared. Indeed, in his treatise he makes use of the very same analogy for which Paley's book is most famous. If one came across a pocket watch, Paley claimed and Roget echoed, one would assume, because of its complexity and its fitness for purpose, the existence of a watchmaker who had designed it. By analogy, the natural world, which showed the same 'manifestation of design', could be assumed to have a creator. However, the future lay with other ideas about the natural world. In the year that Roget's Treatise was published, Charles Darwin was midway through the journey aboard *HMS Beagle* that was to provide him with much of the evidence to support the ideas about natural selection he was to develop. Natural selection and the theory of evolution, as Darwin would reveal in his epoch-making 1859 book *The Origin of Species*, implied that nature needed no intervention by a deity to produce the rich profusion of life that we see around us. The study of natural history, far from providing 'a rich fountain of religious instruction', revealed only the workings of inevitable natural processes. Those looking for 'the Power, Wisdom and Goodness of God as manifested in the Creation' were barking up the wrong tree. Roget's belief, expressed in the very first sentence of his treatise, that 'to investigate the relations which connect Man with his Creator is the noblest exercise of human reason', was sincerely held but, in this context, it was rapidly becoming old-fashioned and outmoded.

The last paragraphs of Roget's treatise suggest that he himself, at some level, was unhappily aware that his view of the world, God's creation and man's place in it might no longer be tenable. He launches upon a series of elaborately constructed rhetorical questions. 'Is Man, the favoured creature of Nature's bounty, the paragon of animals, whose spirit holds communion with celestial powers, formed but to perish with the wreck of his bodily frame? Are generations after generations of his race doomed to follow in endless succession, rolling darkly down the stream of time, and leaving no track in its pathless ocean? Are the operations of Almighty power to end with the present scene?' As he reaches the climax of his rhetoric, Roget makes clear that, for him, the answer is 'No' and that 'there has been vouchsafed to us, from a higher source, a pure and heavenly light to guide our faltering steps, and animate our fainting spirit'. However, there is no mistaking the unspoken fear, lurking beneath the self-consciously wrought prose, that the terrible answer to his questions might just be, 'Yes'. Generations of men might roll darkly down the stream of time and leave no track.

The appalling loss of his wife and the earlier deaths of his father figures Samuel Romilly and Etienne Dumont, who passed away in 1829, must have shaken Roget's faith and forced him to confront his own mortality. In the year after the publication of his Bridgewater Treatise, he was obliged to face another bereavement, although, in this instance, it was one that could not have been entirely unexpected. Over the years the mental health of his mother Catherine Roget had not improved and there had been much talk of the possibility of placing her in some kind of asylum or rest-home. Nothing had ever been decided and she was still being looked after by her long-suffering daughter in Ilfracombe when she died on 6 August 1835. At the time of her death Roget was in Ireland on Royal Society business and needed to travel back on an overnight steam packet. Departing on the evening of 9 August, he arrived in Ilfracombe almost exactly three days later, an indication of the difficulty of making speedy progress in an era before rail travel was widespread. Catherine Roget's life had been, in many ways, a difficult one and its last years had been overshad-owed by the illness, possibly Alzheimer's, which had over-come her but she had lived to see her son, for whom she had sacrificed so much, a man of distinction and achieve-ment. She lies buried in Ilfracombe churchyard. Roget returned to his active and fulfilling life in London. His sister Annette, long accustomed if not reconciled to spin-sterhood, continued to live in the Devon resort.

Meanwhile, Roget's involvement in the day-to-day running of the Royal Society had launched him into further trouble and controversy, this time from a new direction entirely unconnected with Babbage and his concerns about the Society's future. The entire brouhaha was to emerge from what seemed, on the surface, the simplest and most straightforward of projects – producing a new catalogue of the Society's library. Although he had experience himself in such work at the Medical and Chirurgical Society, Roget proposed that Anthony Panizzi, whom he had met socially, should undertake the task. The man Roget proposed, originally christened Antonio Genesio Maria Panizzi, was born in Brescello in the Duchy of Modena in 1797. As a young man he was heavily involved in the political movements to liberalise the reac-tionary states and kingdoms of Italy, many of them ruled by non-Italians, and to bring unity to the Italian nation. He was obliged to flee his native country where he was tried in absentia for his supposed treason, found guilty and (according to some stories) hung in effigy, possibly the only librarian ever to be so treated. After expulsion from a number of other neighbouring states, he arrived as a nearly penniless exile in London in 1823. By 1828, he was Professor of Italian at the newly founded University College, London and three years later he joined the staff of the British Museum library. He was eventually to become principal librarian at the Museum and to be knighted for services to his adopted country.

In view of his later career, Panizzi might have seemed an ideal choice to bring order into the chaos of the library's classification system but the Italian was, throughout his life, a combative and quarrelsome man. Endless arguments developed between him and the committee of the Royal Society that was charged with responsibility for the library and the new catalogue. Despite Roget's attempts to act as peacemaker the battle between Panizzi, a professional librarian who believed he knew best, and the committee, whose members were offended by the Italian's abrasive contempt for their supposed amateurism, grew ever more rancorous. In the end, Panizzi was fired from the job but he retaliated by publishing several pamphlets in which he poured scorn on the Society and its methods. The dispute rumbled on for several years, only finally ending in 1839 when the society quietly agreed to pay Panizzi an extra sum of £328, largely, one imagines, to shut him up.

Other problems, which echoed the concerns raised initially by Babbage and his supporters, continued to dog Roget's career at the Royal Society. Throughout the 1830s, debate centred on the question of papers published in the Society's *Philosophical Transactions* (were there too many of them and were they of sufficiently high a standard?) and on the award of the Society's medals to distinguished scientists (were all the recipients really so distinguished?). With the benefit of hindsight Roget can be seen as being on the 'wrong' side in the debates – a representative of the status quo which was contributing to the fall in the Society's reputation and holding back attempts to make science in Britain more professional and rigorous – but it should be remembered just how much time and effort Roget, in contrast to his critics, was putting in to the actual day-to-day running of the society. It is unsurprising that, immersed as he was in the practicalities of administration, he was unable to see the wider picture.

Typical of the disputes which regularly ruffled the feathers of society fellows and members was the affair of George Newport. Newport was to become a distinguished entomologist and, in his later years, was to be both President of the Entomological Society of London and a correspondent of Charles Darwin but, in the 1830s, he was yet to make his name. It was said that Roget had gained Newport's assistance in the research on his Bridgewater Treatise in return for a promise that the younger man would receive the society's prestigious Royal Medal. One anonymous correspondent in the *Lancet* managed in one concise sentence, not only to impugn Roget's conduct in relation to Newport, but also to accuse him of stealing work from a third party. 'I wish one of your correspondents who is able,' he wrote, 'would show in its true light the affair of the Royal Medal, given by Dr Roget, the plagiarist of Grant, to his friend Newport.' If it was the case that Roget had arranged for Newport to be rewarded with a Royal Society medal, it was undoubtedly a misuse of power but there was little evidence that this was true. Certainly Roget had made use of Newport's work in his Bridgewater Treatise but he had acknowledged this openly and there was no proof that some kind of *quid pro quo* arrangement had been made by the two men. As to the further accusation of plagiarism levelled in the *Lancet*, this also seems to have been based more on malice than evidence. The Grant in question was Robert Edmund Grant, a leading biologist who was to have a major influence on Darwin's work, but again Roget had openly acknowledged that he had drawn on Grant's ideas in his Bridgewater Treatise.

Another dispute which rumbled on for the best part of a decade was that involving the Physiology Committee of the Royal Society, of which Roget was a prominent member, and the surgeons and anatomists Robert Lee and Thomas Snow Beck. This too centred on the controversial award of one of the Society's Royal Medals. Beck received it in 1845 but many reputable people believed that his work, on the nerves of the uterus, was not original and far less deserving of recognition than similar studies by Lee. Lee and his supporters contended that he had been shabbily treated by the Society. It is unnecessary to venture too far into the murky depths of the Lee v. Beck affair. The important point is that it looked once again as if the senior officers of the Society, including Roget, had been prepared to countenance irregularities in the Society's business and then to indulge in what looked remarkably like dishonesty in order to cover up such irregularities.

The whole affair eventually became one of the catalysts for a revolt in the ranks of the society which led to Roget's resignation as Secretary in 1848. It was a post he had held for more than twenty years. This proved the last gasp of the old guard – after the resignation, many of the reformers were elected to positions of power in the society and sweeping changes were made. Roget was replaced by Thomas Bell, a zoologist and anatomist who had been a regular correspondent of Darwin since the young naturalist returned from his voyage on the *Beagle*. The election of the Earl of Rosse as President of the Society in the same year as Roget resigned his post might, at first sight, appear a continuation of the policy of preferring social to scientific status but this was not the case. William Parsons, 3rd Earl of Rosse, as an Irish peer, was not just a long way further down the aristocratic pecking order than the two previous incumbents, the Duke of Sussex and the Marquess of Northampton. He was also an astronomer of real achievement. On his family estates in Ireland he had built what was for a long period the largest telescope in the world, the so-called 'Leviathan of Parsonstown', and he had made a series of pioneering observations through it. It was Rosse, no upper class dilettante but a genuine scientist, who gave the Crab Nebula its name.

From a historical perspective Roget proved once again on the wrong side of the argument. He was clinging to ideas of science and scientific research that had had their day. His opponents were not only largely forgotten figures like Lee. They numbered in their ranks many of the most distinguished men of science of the time, including Sir John Herschel, the astronomer who had been the reformers' candidate for President in 1830, the chemist and physicist William Robert Grove, inventor of the world's first fuel cell, and Sir Charles Lyell, author of *Principles of Geology*, one of the most revolutionary and ground-breaking texts of the nineteenth century. Lyell, particularly exasperated by what he saw as reactionary obscurantism, once described Roget and his associates as 'a set of obstructives, compared to whom Metternich was, I presume, a progressive animal'.

Roget, approaching his seventies, was now seen as an old man holding up the progress of science and its more youthful and dynamic practitioners. To the likes of Herschel, Grove and Lyell, he was a relic from the past. It was time to step aside, as he himself recognised. In his resignation speech to the Royal Society, he acknowledged that, 'Having now grown grey in that service, I feel that it is time for me to retire, while my strength is yet unbroken, and before the changes which the Society is now undergoing shall cause fresh demands to be made upon it...' Yet he was not going to depart without a parting shot or two at his opponents. In the same speech, he also spoke of 'a series of malignant attacks, carried on with extraordinary pertinacity during nearly two years, against the Society, its President, and above all, the Committee of Physiology; and these attacks were pointed more particularly against myself, under the erroneous notion that I was especially responsible for the proceedings of that committee'. He was clear, however, that the time had come for him to go. 'While the battle was raging,' he said, 'I could not, in honour, withdraw from the field; my duty was to remain at my post and abide the pelting of the storm. But these squalls having now blown over, I feel at liberty to retreat, and to resign into your hands the trust you have so long and so liberally confided to me.' Roget's long career as an officer of the society was over.

Roget and his Thesaurus

'The man is not wholly evil – he has a Thesaurus in his cabin.'

(description of Captain Hook
in JM Barrie's *Peter Pan*)

It is ironic that Roget is remembered today, not for any of his medical or scientific achievements, but for the compilation of a linguistic work of reference. However, throughout his career and from at least 1805 onwards, he had been drawing up, for his own interest and use, lists of words arranged in particular orders. Indeed, one of the very earliest of Roget's notebooks to survive dates from 1787, when he was eight years old, and contains lists of Latin words, with English translations, all divided up into subject areas like 'Beasts', 'People' and 'Parts of the Body'. Of course, it is the kind of list that thousands of schoolboys over the centuries have compiled and does not indicate a precocious awareness of what his future work was to be but it is a pleasing coincidence that some of the first pages to survive in Roget's handwriting consist of a themed list of words.

However, real work on what was to become the

Thesaurus did begin when he was a young man, as he himself tells us. 'It is now nearly fifty years,' he wrote in the preface to the first edition of his Thesaurus, 'since I first projected a system of verbal classification similar to that on which the present work is founded. Conceiving that such a compilation might help to supply my own deficiencies, I had, in the year 1805, completed a classed catalogue of words on a small scale, but on the same principle, and nearly in the same form, as the Thesaurus now published.' It was all part of his desire, so typical of the man and of his era, to classify knowledge and bring it under human control. Freed from his troublesome and often tiresome responsibilities at the Royal Society and released from the coils of the many controversies which had swirled about his head, Roget was able to give serious thought to what became his *Thesaurus* or, to give it its more extensive title, his *Thesaurus of English Words and Phrases So Classified and Arranged as to Facilitate the Expression of Ideas and Assist in Literary Composition*. 'I had often... found this little collection [his 1805 catalogue], scanty and imperfect though it was, of much use to me in literary composition, and often contemplated its extension and improvement; but a sense of the magnitude of the task, amidst a multiple of other avocations, deterred me from the attempt.' Now its time had arrived.

Roget's only previous writing on a literary subject was an article on Dante in the *Edinburgh Review* in 1818 which he co-wrote with the exiled Italian poet Ugo Foscolo and it is likely that it was the Italian who provided most of the expertise in this venture, Roget merely helping to express Foscolo's ideas in English. There is little evidence to show that Roget's reading included much imaginative literature. Given the sheer volume of scientific work he did, and the amount of reading of scientific papers and texts that he would have had to undertake, he would have had little extra time for poetry or fiction. Roget's interest in language, as befitted a practising scientist, was purely utilitarian. He was interested in 'style' only in so far as it enabled the clear expression of ideas and thoughts and the lucid description of experiments and inventions. When he criticised a particular paper submitted to the Royal Society, it was for its 'want of perspicuity and precision' and the fact that its author's 'meaning is often obscured by a diffuseness and laxity of expression, rendering it difficult to follow the course of his argument' rather than for any lack of literary graces.

As his biographer DL Emblen rightly states, Roget's 'real intellectual gift and joy was the ability to bring about order in that which lacked it'. In this sense, despite the fact that he possessed no particular expertise in language and literature, Roget was the ideal man to create the Thesaurus. As a modern editor of the Thesaurus has pointed out, bringing order in that which lacked it also helped to soothe Roget's own personal anxieties about the fast-changing world in which he was growing old. 'Not only did the *Thesaurus* utilize all Roget's competences,' Betty Kirkpatrick wrote in an introduction to her 1998 edition, 'it also fulfilled a need for him: the need, in a society changing with frightening speed, where the old moral and religious order was increasingly in question, to reaffirm order, stability and unity, and through them the purpose of a universal, supernatural authority.' Writing his Bridgewater Treatise had not eased Roget's unconscious anxieties. Perhaps, the creation of his Thesaurus would.

Roget had high expectations of his book. In his own eyes he was not creating just a work of reference, to be consulted by writers hoping to extend their vocabulary and ornament their style. He was providing the basis for a rigorous philosophy of language, a guide even to the ultimate classification of human knowledge. 'Metaphysicians engaged in the more profound investigation of the Philosophy of Language will be materially assisted by having the ground thus prepared for them, in a previous analysis and classification of our ideas; for such classification of ideas is the true basis on which words, which are their symbols, should be classified. It is by such analysis alone that we can arrive at a clear perception of the relation which these symbols bear to their corresponding ideas...' He was, in his own estimation, endeavouring to formulate the principles on which 'a strictly Philosophical Language might be constructed', even perhaps taking the first steps which would eventually lead towards the realisation of 'that splendid aspiration of philanthropists – the establishment of a Universal Language'. What he could not imagine he was doing was creating a *vade mecum* for generations of crossword puzzlers as yet unborn.

In creating the Thesaurus, Roget was drawing on the knowledge of science and scientific thinking he had gained over the decades. The book attempts to impose on language the same kind of system of classification that, say, Linnaeus had placed upon natural history. Words are divided into categories in much the same way that, in the Linnaean taxonomy, plants and animals are divided into families and genera. Just as a genus can then be subdivided into smaller groupings, consisting of a number of individual but related species, so can words be classified into ever smaller categories in which the individual units (the words) are linked through closeness of meaning. Thus, Roget begins with what he calls his 'six primary classes of category' (Abstract Relations, Space, Material World, Intellect, Volition and Sentient and Moral Powers) and then gradually, through a descending order of sections and subsections, he focuses in on individual words. The six 'primary classes' can be seen as analogous to 'phyla' in zoological classification, the next layer of sections to what are called classes in zoology and so on. Roget is quite explicit about the link with natural history. 'The principle by which I have been guided in framing my verbal classification,' he writes, 'is the same as that which is employed in the various departments of natural history. Thus the sectional divisions I have formed correspond to natural families in botany and zoology, and the filiation of words presents a network analogous to the natural filiation of plants or animals.'

The Thesaurus was not, by any means, the first

compilation to attempt some kind of categorisation of language. In his introduction to the first edition, Roget himself drew attention to a Sanskrit work, 'supposed to be at least nine hundred years old', known as the *Amarakosha*. It may seem odd that the *Amarakosha* had come to Roget's attention but an English translation had been published in India in 1808 and he must have seen it. Certainly he knew enough about it to criticise it. Although he was prepared to admit that it was 'a remarkable effort at analysis at so remote a period of Indian literature', Roget was dismissive of the *Amarakosha*'s classification system which he snootily described as 'exceedingly imperfect and confused, especially in all that relates to abstract ideas or mental operations'.

Nearer both in time and place, and also mentioned by Roget, was *An Essay Towards a Real Character and a Philosophical Language* by John Wilkins, one of the leading intellectuals in mid-seventeenth century England. Although he had blotted his royalist copybook by marrying Oliver Cromwell's sister Robina during the Commonwealth years, Wilkins was none the less made Bishop of Chester in the reign of Charles II. One of Roget's predecessors as Secretary of the Royal Society (indeed, he was one of the Society's founding members and its first Secretary), the bishop was an adventurous thinker who believed, among other things, that the moon was habitable and that men would one day travel there. His essay on language appeared in 1668 and was an examination of its subject in four parts. Its first part considered how languages and alphabets had originated. The second part, which was the section of the work that most clearly influenced Roget, provided a classification of ideas and words. The third and fourth parts looked at grammar and syntax and elaborated Wilkins' own notions of a possible universal language. Although he clearly admired Wilkins' work, Roget had serious reservations about its usefulness. 'It professed to be founded on a scheme of analysis of the things or notions to which names were to be assigned,' he wrote, 'but notwithstanding the immense labour and ingenuity expended in the construction of this system, it was soon found to be far too abstruse and recondite for practical application.'

More recently still, others had attempted to produce books that were not ambitious philosophical tracts like *An Essay Towards a Real Character and a Philosophical Language* but simply guides to English synonyms. Hester Lynch Piozzi, better known under her previous married name as Dr. Johnson's friend, Mrs Thrale, published *British Synonymy; or, an Attempt at Regulating the Choice of Words in Familiar Conversation* in Dublin in 1794. Married to an Italian musician, Mrs Piozzi was more concerned with helping the 'foreign friends' she mentions in her book's dedication in their attempts to grapple with the complexities of correctly spoken English than she was in systematic analysis of the language. George Crabb, a lawyer who had become a prolific and versatile author, published *English Synonymes Explained* in 1816. Thirty-five years later – only the year before Roget published his work – Crabb's volume was still being described as 'the only full and explanatory book of the kind we possess' but it lacked most of the organisational structure of the Thesaurus. Indeed there had been more than twenty previous such reference works in English but none had had anything like the ambition and range of Roget's.

Why was the book called a Thesaurus? It was a word that Roget himself chose for his work of reference, derived ultimately from an ancient Greek word meaning a 'treasure house'. During the Renaissance, it had been regularly employed as a synonym for 'dictionary' or 'word list' but it had long fallen into disuse when Roget resurrected it for his own work. Roget's Thesaurus was to be a treasure house of language which writers and scholars could visit in search of the particular gems they required.

Roget was just as clear about what his work of reference was not meant to be. The purpose of the book, he noted, 'is not to explain the signification of words, but simply to classify and arrange them according to the sense in which they are now used, and which I presume to be already known to the reader'. 'Far less do I venture,' he went on, 'to thrid the mazes of the vast labyrinth into which I should be led by any attempt at a general discrimination of synonyms.' As he confessed with what one can sense was real feeling, 'The difficulties I have had to contend with have already been sufficiently great, without this addition to my labours.'

Previous attempts at dictionaries of English synonyms had often been as much concerned with laying down the law on how words *should* be used as with describing precisely how they were. Both the work by Mrs Piozzi, as its subtitle implies, and Crabb's book, the most popular guide to synonyms before the publication of the Thesaurus, had attempted to impose rules on the use of language and the validity of particular words. Roget was not interested in issuing such dictatorial mandates and, in his introduction, he found his own typically long-winded way of saying his Thesaurus was descriptive rather than prescriptive: 'With regard to the admission of many words and expressions, which the classical reader might be disposed to condemn as vulgarisms, or which he perhaps might stigmatize as usage of the day, I would beg to observe, that, having due regard to the uses to which this Work was to be adapted, I did not feel myself justified in excluding them solely on that ground, if they possessed an acknowledged currency in general intercourse.'

He was, however, concerned with the ways in which imprecise use of language reflected shoddy and irrational thinking. 'False logic,' he wrote, 'disguised under specious phraseology, too often gains the assent of the unthinking multitude, disseminating far and wide the seeds of prejudice and error. Truisms pass current, and wear the semblance of profound wisdom, when dressed up in the tinsel garb of antithetical phrases, or set off by an imposing pomp of paradox. By a confused jargon of involved and mystical sentences, the imagination is easily inveigled into the belief that it is acquiring knowledge and approaching truth.' His Thesaurus, he believed, could be a powerful weapon in the war against imprecision, pretentiousness and the clumsy use of language.

Four years after his departure from the Royal Society, Roget's Thesaurus was ready for publication. The original agreement he made with the publishers Longman, Brown, Green and Longmans, dated 17 January 1852, was for an edition of a thousand copies and, after deducting costs, profits were to be divided equally between Roget and the publisher. The retail price was to be 14 shillings and the book duly appeared in the spring of 1852. It was not the only classic work to appear that year. In March, Charles Dickens began to publish *Bleak House* in monthly parts, one of his finest and most comprehensive panoramas of nineteenth-century English society. *Uncle Tom's Cabin*, Harriet Beecher Stowe's eye-opening indictment of the cruelties of slavery, also appeared in 1852 as did Thackeray's historical novel *Henry Esmond* and *The Blithedale Romance* by Nathaniel Hawthorne. The Thesaurus took its place alongside such volumes on the shelves of the nation's booksellers.

Like so many classic works, the Thesaurus was not immediately and universally acclaimed. 'This is at least a curious book,' wrote one reviewer, apparently slightly baffled by the volume in front of him, 'novel in its design, most laboriously wrought, but, we fear, not likely to be so practically useful as the care and toil and thought bestowed upon it might have deserved.' Another was equally concerned that Roget had expended huge amounts of effort to little ultimate purpose. 'The labour of getting up such a work as this must have been enormous,' he wrote, 'but will its usefulness repay the toil by profit as much as its ingenuity will entitle him to honour?' Some reviewers did, however, understand what Roget was trying to do. A writer in the *Westminster Review*, which had been founded by Roget's old collaborator, now long since dead, Jeremy Bentham, prophesied (quite correctly) that, 'Roget will rank with Samuel Johnson as a literary instrument-maker of the first class'.

Although it was consistently and regularly reprinted, sales of the Thesaurus in the nineteenth century were not such that it would today be considered a bestseller. The original one thousand copies presumably sold, since Longmans produced a second edition in March 1853 of fifteen hundred. For this edition, the author was to receive not half the profits but two thirds. After that, sales during Roget's lifetime seem to have been relatively stable. About a thousand sold each year, although Longman were slow to realise what a goldmine they had on their lists and continued to be conservative in the numbers they printed. The seventh reprinting, in September 1858, consisted of just 250 copies.

In the last decades of the nineteenth century, the Thesaurus became a Roget family business. Roget himself saw nearly thirty reprints of the book come off the presses before his death, most of them with additions and corrections he had made. According to one, possibly apocryphal, report he was working on the twenty-eighth edition on the evening before the day he died. His son, John Lewis

Roget, oversaw dozens more revised editions until he died in 1908 whereupon the grandson of the original Roget, Samuel Romilly Roget, carried on the work until his death in 1952, exactly one hundred years after the original publication of the Thesaurus. Throughout this century of Roget, Longmans continued to be the publishers and it was this firm which eventually bought out the rights from the family.

The Thesaurus has had almost as long a publishing history in America as it has had in Britain. The first American edition of the Thesaurus appeared only a few years after the original English one and was edited by a man named Barnas Sears. Sears was a distinguished Massachussetts educationalist who went on to become the President of Brown University. He was also a puritanical busybody who omitted from his edition of Roget what he thought were vulgar words and phrases and then made matters worse by putting them back into subsequent editions but in a separate appendix. Thus the words and phrases Sears had considered potentially corrupting, including such unlikely ones as 'fiddle-faddle', 'a wild goose chase' and 'a cock and bull story', were all gathered together in one easily accessible place. In the 1880s the publishing firm of Thomas Y. Crowell and Company took over responsibility for producing the American version of the Thesaurus and theirs were the standard editions on the other side of the Atlantic for many years.

As the twentieth century dawned, Roget's Thesaurus, already half a century old, was still selling as well as it had

ever done and was on the way to developing into the institution it has now become. Revised editions, produced
first by Roget's now elderly son and then by his grandson,
continued to appear. However, as the century went on to
enter its second and third decades, a new impetus was
given to its sales. The crossword craze hit America and the
rest of the world and Roget proved to be the ideal reference work for baffled puzzlers everywhere.

Arthur Wynne was a Liverpool-born journalist and
compiler of puzzles who emigrated to the USA. In 1913,
he was working for the *New York World* when his editor
asked him to create a new puzzle for the newspaper's
'Sunday Fun' section. Wynne remembered a game from
his English childhood called 'Magic Squares' in which a
given group of words had to be arranged so that they read
the same both horizontally and vertically. Devising a
diamond-shaped grid and providing clues to the words
rather than just supplying them, he came up with what he
called originally a 'word-cross' puzzle that was published
in the *New York World* on 21 December 1913. Wynne's new
puzzle caught on immediately and other newspapers
began to publish similar ones.

By 1924, when the first book of what were by then
called crosswords was published by Simon and Schuster,
the novelty puzzle had become a nationwide craze.
Crossword tournaments were organised. (Yale defeated
Harvard in one of the earliest such contests in 1925.)
Railroads printed crosswords on the backs of their dining
room menus. At a fashion show, a designer unveiled

dresses with crosswords embroidered on them and offered discounts on future purchases to those who could solve them. Jeremiahs in the newspapers predicted devastating social consequences from the nation's obsession with crosswords and calculated that five million manhours a day were being wasted in 'unprofitable trifling'. Whatever the consequences for the American nation, the results for the publishers of *Roget's Thesaurus* were entirely beneficial. Sales soared almost overnight in the year Simon and Schuster published the first crossword book. A writer in the *New York Times* in 1925, with somewhat forced jocularity, took note of the new importance of Roget's work. 'The victim of crosswordophobia first called in the dictionary and that alleviated his suffering a little. But something more potent was demanded by many of the complications that developed, and the Thesaurus proved the efficacious poultice for his aching brow. In homes where a few weeks ago volume and compiler were not even names, the book has found a place where in the Age of Innocence the family Bible might have rested.' When the crossword craze crossed the Atlantic and reached Britain, similar increases in sales were recorded. In the decades since then, the Thesaurus has gone from strength to strength. It is difficult to calculate numbers exactly but it is likely that in excess of thirty million copies of Roget's reference work have now been sold.

Yet, despite its success, there have always been those who understand the purpose of the Thesaurus but either disapprove of that purpose or deplore the effects on language that they assume will follow from regular use of Roget's work. Soon after it was published, a critic in *The North American Review* made mock of it and questioned the uses to which it could be put. 'If it does nothing else,' the anonymous reviewer wrote, 'it will bring a popular theory to the test; and if that theory be correct, we count upon witnessing a mob of mute Miltons and Bacons, and speechless Chathams and Burkes, crowding and tramping into print. Dr. Roget, for a moderate fee, prescribes the verbal medicine which will relieve the congestion of their thoughts. All the tools and implements employed by all the poets and philosophers of England can be obtained at his shop. The idea being given, he guarantees in every case to supply the word.'

The Thesaurus has come under fire more recently as well. In a long article written for *The Atlantic Monthly* in May 2001, entitled 'Roget and His Brilliant, Unrivaled, Malign, and Detestable Thesaurus', Simon Winchester, author of a book on the history of the *Oxford English Dictionary*, questioned the validity of Roget's work and claimed that it had become little more than a crutch for the intellectually and linguistically challenged. Although prepared to admit that Roget was possessed of a 'nobly Platonic vision.... that the language could come to be seen as an ordered part of the cosmos, amply reflective of divine will and inspiration', Winchester was in no doubt that the influence of his great work had, in practice, been a malign one. '*Roget*,' he wrote, 'has become no more than a calculator for the lexically lazy: used too often, relied on at all, it will cause the most valuable part of the brain to atrophy, the core of human expression to wither.' The novelist Lawrence Norfolk, in an article in *The Guardian* of 13 July 2002, was similarly sceptical of the value of the book. 'The chicken-and-egg relationship between language and thought bedevils *Roget's Thesaurus*,' he wrote. 'The category of people who know what they want to say but not how to say it is vanishingly small. Those who know neither what they want to say nor how to say it are more numerous, but probably beyond help. The great irony of Roget is that this most usable of books has no obvious use.' A century and a half after its first publication, the Thesaurus proved able still to arouse controversy as the response to Winchester's article in particular (dozens of impassioned letters in defence of Roget were despatched to the offices of *The Atlantic Monthly*) showed.

Roget's Last Years

In the last two decades of his long life, Roget was almost as busy as he had ever been. He oversaw not only the frequent new editions of the Thesaurus but new editions of his other works. Although his Bridgewater Treatise, seen with hindsight, appears old-fashioned, it had proved successful enough and, even in 1867, eight years after the publication of Darwin's *The Origin of Species*, a further edition, the fourth, was produced. At the age of eighty-eight, Roget provided extra material for it. He also maintained his membership of a large array of intellectual and scientific societies from the Medical and Chirurgical Society, which he had first joined in 1808, to the Royal Society itself. In some of these societies, he continued to hold official positions even after he had resigned from his secretaryship at the Royal Society. He was still a Vice-President of the Royal Society of Arts, for example, three years after the first publication of the Thesaurus.

He devoted time to chess. It was a game by which he had long been fascinated and he had, in the past, written papers on it with such typically long-winded Rogetian titles as 'Description of a Method of Moving the Knight over Every Square of the Chess-board Without Going

Twice over Any One; Commencing at Any Given Square, and Ending at Any Other Given Square of a Different Colour'. (The so-called 'Knight's Tour' is an old chess puzzle, which devotees of the game have pondered for centuries. Roget's paper provides his own solution, one of many devised over the years.) He had also created chess puzzles for magazines and newspapers such as *The Illustrated London News*. In 1845, Roget had even attempted to market a travelling chess set of his own devising. The 'Economic Chess-board', usually recognised by historians of the game as the first ever pocket chess set, was the result of his irritation at not being able to play the game when he was travelling. It was not a financial success but, within little more than a decade, other pocket chess-boards had been created and they had become a familiar sight in Victorian England.

There are other glimpses of Roget as an old man. In 1852, from his new home in Upper Bedford Place, he writes to the artist William Brockedon (who, twenty years earlier, had created one of the few surviving portraits of Roget, a chalk drawing now in the National Portrait Gallery) and thanks him for his assistance in election to yet another society, the Graphic Society. Five years later, he was one of the many subscribers to a fund raised by Lady Jane Franklin to finance another expedition to the Arctic in search of her husband who had disappeared in the icy wastes of northern Canada more than a decade earlier. Any animus Lady Franklin may once have felt towards her old flame had clearly vanished. Roget had been very ill and she was now concerned only with singing his praises. 'How truly characteristic it is in this man,' she wrote in her journal, 'rising from a bed which threatened to be his last, and again in the world.' In that same year, an American visitor to London, the pioneering woman astronomer Maria Mitchell, was introduced at a scientific gathering to 'a fine-looking, white-headed, good-featured old man' who 'was Roget of the "Thesaurus".'

In 1858, we even find Roget embroiled briefly in the kind of dispute that had enlivened his time as Secretary of the Royal Society. Many years earlier, one of the many articles he had contributed to the *Encyclopaedia Britannica* had been on the subject of the deaf and the dumb. Nearly forty years on, the eighth edition of *Britannica* reprinted Roget's article much as it had been written and one reader, the principal of a school for the deaf and dumb in Liverpool, was moved to complain. He published a pamphlet in which he lambasted the *Britannica* entry and pointed out 'the most ludicrous errors of fact' that it contained, including references to men as alive who had been dead for decades. Wisely, Roget, now nearly eighty years old, decided not to respond himself but to leave it to the new publishers of *Britannica*, Adam and Charles Black, to defend his work. They did the best they could but the truth was that the critic was largely correct. The article was out of date and should not have been reprinted as it stood.

His children had now, of course, grown up. His son,

John Lewis Roget, had trained as a lawyer at Cambridge and Lincoln's Inn Fields but his abiding interest was in art. He became a well-known watercolour painter who went on to publish both collections of his own work and a two-volume *History of the Old Watercolour Society*, a record of the activities of what became the Royal Watercolour Society. John Lewis provided assistance to his father on the last editions of the Thesaurus to be published before 1869 and inherited the responsibility for it on his father's death. Roget's daughter, Kate, never married and became the companion of his old age, looking after the home in Upper Bedford Place to which he had moved in 1843.

In a couplet written in a letter of 1859, Roget noted that:

> Time wastes us all, our bodies and our wits;
> But we waste time – so Time and we are quits

It was not a sentiment that could be applied to Roget himself. He had never been one to waste time and, apart from an increasing deafness, he was, even in his eighties, a healthy and vigorous man. The publisher Charles Knight recorded a meeting with him in 1863 and described him as 'full of animation, with undimmed intelligence'. In the autumn of the following year, Roget was sturdy enough to make a trip into the West Country to attend the annual meeting of the British Association for the Advancement of Science.

However, time took its toll on those he knew and those

he loved. In 1866, his younger sister Annette died in Ilfracombe at the age of eighty-three. In death, as in life, Annette has been unable to escape her mother. She is buried beside her in the Ilfracombe churchyard. In August 1867, the last and probably the greatest of the scientists who might be considered Roget's contemporaries, Michael Faraday, died in his house in Hampton. Even Faraday was twelve years younger than Roget. Some men from the past, including long-time opponents like Charles Babbage and the geologist Charles Lyell, still survived but the world and the people that Roget had known for so long were now largely gone.

In the late summer of 1869, aged ninety, he left London, as he had done for a number of years, for a short stay in the Worcestershire village of West Malvern. The Malvern Hills and the spa at Malvern were a popular destination with those seeking to take the waters and restore their health. Accompanied by his unmarried daughter Kate, Roget took rooms in a house there and it was there, after a short illness, that he died on 12 September 1869. According to the obituary that was published in the *Proceedings of the Royal Society* the following year, he left the world 'peacefully and without suffering, from the natural decay of that vital power, the mysterious working of which he had so laboured to illustrate'. Peter Mark Roget is buried in the churchyard of St. James's Church in West Malvern. His gravestone is a simple one and bears no inscription beyond the basic details of name, date and place of death and the age at which he died. Of all the various honours that were accorded to him in his lifetime, the only two that he wished to be recorded on his gravestone were, significantly, his degree of MD and the letters FRS which denoted membership of the Society that had meant so much to him.

Roget had lived so long that there were few people left to mourn him who remembered him from his pre-Thesaurus days. Lady Jane Franklin, once the Jane Griffin who had had dreams of marrying him and now the seventy-eight-year-old widow of a national hero, recorded his passing in her journal. 'What memories!', she noted as she cut and pasted an obituary from *The Times* into it. For others, his name was one from the distant past. Many may have believed that he had died years earlier.

What should our final view of Roget be? He was not, like some of the men he knew, a great scientist. He was not a great experimenter like Humphry Davy and Michael Faraday nor a visionary such as his old opponent Charles Babbage. Indeed, in many of the debates which characterised nineteenth-century science, Roget was on what future generations have come to see as the losing side. In many ways, he was more representative of the old eighteenth-century idea of the gentleman amateur in science than of the new notion of the professional scientist. Yet, as we have seen, his achievements were many and varied.

The paradox of Roget's long and productive life is that, the very point when he seemed to have been left behind, when he had resigned from the Royal Society and allowed younger men to take over, was the moment when he began work on what was to prove his greatest triumph and his greatest gift to posterity. Over the many decades since his death, Roget the man has largely been hidden behind Roget the book. So powerful an influence on English-speaking culture has the Thesaurus become that 'Roget' has been transformed into shorthand for a particular type of reference work. Ask the average librarian or bookseller or just a general reader for a 'Roget' and he or she will instantly know what is wanted. This short book has attempted to rescue Peter Mark Roget from the curious fate of being lost behind the startling success of his greatest achievement. There was much more to Roget than just his Thesaurus and the man who became a book deserves to be remembered not just as the maker of a classic reference work but as one of the most remarkable men of his era.

Further Reading

Emblen, DL, *Peter Mark Roget: The Word and the Man*, London: Longman, 1970

The standard biography of Roget, still unmatched nearly forty years after its first publication.

Gwynn, Robin D., *Huguenot Heritage*, Eastbourne: Sussex Academic Press, 2000

A book which charts the contributions of the Huguenot exiles to British life.

Hall, Marie Boas, *All Scientists Now: The Royal Society in the Nineteenth Century*, Cambridge: Cambridge University Press, 1984

A scholarly history including details of Roget's period as Secretary and the arguments and debates which characterised it.

Hamilton, James, *Faraday: The Life*, London: HarperCollins, 2002

The most recent biography of one of Roget's greatest contemporaries.

Holder, RW, *The Dictionary Men*, Bath: Bath University Press, 2004

A collection of biographical sketches of lexicographers, including Roget, Dr Johnson and Noah Webster.

Hüllen, Werner, *A History of Roget's Thesaurus*, Oxford: Oxford University Press, 2004

Written by an academic at the University of Duisburg-Essen in Germany, this is a detailed linguistic study of the structure of the Thesaurus and of its historical antecedents.

Hylton, Stuart, *A History of Manchester*, Chichester: Phillimore, 2003

A one-volume history of the city which is particularly good on its transformation into an industrial powerhouse and on the early years of the nineteenth century when Roget was living there.

Knight, David, *Humphry Davy: Science and Power*, Cambridge: Cambridge University Press, 1996

A biography of Davy which includes a chapter on his time at the Pneumatic Institution.

McGoogan, Frank, *Lady Franklin's Revenge*, London: Transworld, 2006

A biography of Lady Jane Franklin which includes a section on her relationship with Roget.

Swade, Doron, *The Cogwheel Brain*, London: Little, Brown, 2000

The story of Charles Babbage and his attempts to build a calculating machine.

Websites

www.rain.org/~karpeles/rogfrm.html
The website of the Karpeles Manuscript Library has a small archive of Roget's manuscripts online including an original manuscript of the Thesaurus.

http://mizian.com.ne.kr/englishwiz/library/rog/index.htm
An online version of the Thesaurus together with Roget's original 1852 introduction.

www.royalsoc.ac.uk
The website of the society to which Roget gave so much of his time includes information about its history in the nineteenth century.

http://en.wikipedia.org/wiki/Peter_Roget
The online entry on Roget in Wikipedia includes some basic information on his life and a number of interesting links.

www.manchester2002-uk.com/celebs/scientists2.html
A site about famous Mancunians which includes information about Roget and colleagues in Manchester like Ferriar and Dalton.

Index

Africa, 15, 39

American War of
Independence, 12

Ampère, Andre Marie, 71

*An Account of the Disease
lately prevalent at the
General Penitentiary*, 84

anatomy, 12, 20, 49, 50,
76

*Animal and Vegetable
Physiology Considered with
Reference to Natural
Theology*, 109

Babbage, Charles, 13, 104,
105, 106, 107, 108,
115, 116, 143, 144

Beck, Thomas Snow, 118

Bell, Thomas, 119

Bentham, Jeremy, 13, 29,
30, 31, 81, 133

Bostock, John, 52, 92

Brewster, David, 20, 94,
108

Bridgewater Treatise, 111,
112, 114, 117, 118,
126, 139

Britain, 11, 12, 15, 29, 43,
48, 75, 117, 134, 136

British Association for the
Advancement of
Science, 67, 108, 109,
142

Buckland, William, 110,
111

Coleridge, Samuel Taylor,
13, 24, 25, 27, 28

Combe, George, 77, 79,
80

*Conversations on Natural
Philiosophy*, 54

Cook, Captain, 15

Crabb, George, 129, 131

Cummings, John, 53

Dalton, John, 44, 45
Daniell, John Frederic, 60, 71
Darwin, Charles, 20, 57, 80, 112, 117, 118, 119, 139
Davy, Humphry, 13, 25, 55, 107, 144
Dickens, Charles, 78, 132
Dumont, Etienne, 29, 33, 41, 49, 65, 92, 93, 114

Edgeworth, Lovell, 23, 36, 39, 93
Edinburgh, 19, 20, 21, 22, 29, 36, 41, 50, 52, 76, 77, 106, 124
education, 12, 18, 42, 69, 70, 109
electricity, 70
Elliotson, John, 78
Emblen, DL, 13, 46, 84, 85, 125
Encyclopaedia Britannica, 32, 67, 68, 69, 76, 77, 79, 94, 141

England, 17, 35, 37, 40, 41, 55, 63, 72, 100, 108, 128, 137, 140

Faraday, Michael, 13, 54, 55, 57, 71, 96, 97, 98, 143, 144
Feinagle, Gregor von, 57, 58
Ferriar, John, 43, 85
France, 16, 35, 36, 37, 39, 54, 99, 105
Franklin, Sir John, 91, 140, 144
French Revolution, 24, 36
Frigidarium, 30, 31, 81
Fuller, John, 55, 56, 57

Gall, Franz Joseph, 75, 79
galvanism, 12, 70
Geneva, 16, 17, 18, 29, 36, 37, 38, 39, 52
George III, 15, 55, 81, 108
George IV, 85
Georgian period, 12
Griffin, Jane, 91, 144
Grove, William Robert, 120

Henry, Thomas, 44, 132

Herschel, John, 106, 107, 108, 119, 120

Hobson, Jonathan, 92

Hobson, Mary Taylor, 92, 93, 99, 100, 101

House of Commons, 56, 63, 83

Ilfracombe, 41, 46, 88, 89, 90, 93, 114, 143

industrial revolution, 15, 33

kaleidoscope, 20, 68, 94, 108

Knight, Charles, 70, 142

Lancet, 117, 118

Lansdowne, Lord, 41

Latham, Peter Mere, 81, 82, 83, 84, 85

Lee, Robert, 118, 119

London, 15, 16, 17, 23, 28, 29, 31, 32, 37, 41, 42, 47, 49, 50, 51, 52, 54, 57, 60, 65, 66, 67, 70, 71, 76, 78, 79, 85, 87, 88, 90, 91, 101, 104, 114, 115, 117, 140, 141, 143

Lyell, Charles, 13, 120, 143

magnetism, 12, 70, 72

Manchester, 22, 33, 41, 42, 43, 44, 45, 46, 47, 85, 92

Marcet, Alexander, 52, 53, 54, 64, 66, 72, 73, 80

mathematics, 12, 44, 70

Medical and Chirurgical Society, 51, 52, 53, 54, 72, 78, 83, 92, 115, 139

Medical Society of London, 51, 52

mesmerism, 78

Millbank Penitentiary, 81, 82, 84

Monty Python's Flying Circus, 11

natural philosophy, 44, 104

Newport, George, 117, 118

North America, 15

Ohm, Georg Simon, 71

Origin of Species, The, 80,

112, 139

Ørsted, Hans Christian, 71

Paley, William, 112
Panizzi, Anthony, 115, 116
Pasteur, Louis, 85
Peter Mark Roget: The Man and the Word, 13
Phenakistoscope, 97, 98
Philips, John, 33, 34, 42
phrenology, 68, 75, 76, 77, 78, 80
physiology, 12, 55, 57, 68, 118, 120
Piozzi, Hester Lynch, 129, 131
Plateau, Joseph, 97, 98

Roget, Annette, 17, 18, 32, 46, 47, 88, 89, 90, 93, 115, 143
Roget, Catherine, 16, 17, 18, 21, 22, 29, 46, 49, 88, 89, 93, 99, 100, 114
Roget, Jean, 16, 17
Roget, John Lewis, 99, 133, 142
Roget, Mary Taylor, 101
Roget's Thesaurus, 11, 124,

125, 130, 132, 134, 136, 138
Romilly, Anne, 64, 65
Romilly, Samuel, 16, 17, 20, 29, 33, 45, 47, 63, 64, 65, 66, 72, 88, 114, 134
Royal Institution, 54, 55, 56, 57, 68, 81, 85, 91, 96
Royal Society, 12, 26, 44, 51, 58, 59, 93, 94, 95, 103, 105, 106, 108, 109, 114, 115, 116, 117, 118, 120, 124, 125, 128, 132, 139, 141, 143, 145
Royal Society of Arts, 60, 139

SDUK/Society for the Diffusion of Useful Knowledge, 69, 70
South, Sir James, 106
Stampfer, Simon von, 97, 98
Switzerland, 17, 37, 38, 54
Tennyson, Alfred Lord, 104, 105

Thesaurus, 11, 58, 68,
99, 123, 124, 125,
127, 130, 131, 132,
133, 134, 136, 137,
139, 141, 142, 144, 145

Victoria, Queen, 15, 82
Victorian era, 12, 103
visual perception, 12, 97

Watt, James, 13, 23, 33
Wilkins, John, 128, 129
Wordsworth, William, 13,
24, 25
Wynne, Arthur, 135

Yelloly, John, 52

zoology, 69, 127

OTHER TITLES IN THIS SERIES

Alchemy and Alchemists	Sean Martin	978-1-904048-62-6
Conspiracy Theories	Robin Ramsay	978-1-904048-65-7
Jack The Ripper	Mark Whitehead & Miriam Rivett	978-1-904048-69-5
Nazi War Trials	Andrew Walker	978-1-903047-50-7
Nelson	Victoria Carolan	978-1-904048-54-1
Psychogeography	Merlin Coverley	978-1-904048-61-7
Secret Societies	Nick Harding	978-1-904048-41-1
St. George	Giles Morgan	978-1-904048-57-2
The Cathars	Sean Martin	978-1-904048-33-6
The Crusades	Mike Paine	978-1-904048-38-1
The Gnostics	Sean Martin	978-1-904048-56-5
The Holy Grail	Giles Morgan	978-1-904048-34-X
The Knights Templar	Sean Martin	978-1-904048-28-2
The Universe	Richard Osborne	978-1-904048-82-4

All available in distinctive hardcover volumes at £9.99

www.pocketessentials.com